ZOMBIES from History

GEOFF HOLDER

To Cate, who came up with the idea.

For more on the strange and grotesque books written
by the author, go to www.geoffholder.com

First published 2013

The History Press
The Mill, Brimscombe Port
Stroud, Gloucestershire, GL5 2QG
www.thehistorypress.co.uk

British Library Cataloguing in Publication Data.
A catalogue record for this book is available from the British Library.

ISBN 978 0 7524 9964 2

Typesetting and origination by The History Press
Printed in Great Britain by CPI Group (UK) Ltd, Croydon, CR0 4YY

CONTENTS

Introduction ⸻ 7

Anti-Zombie Weapons ⸻ 10

Defending the Body ⸻ 13

Zombies from History ⸻ 15

including Britain's Best Anti-Zombie Castles ⸻ 54

Bibliography ⸻ 180

Zombie Credits ⸻ 185

Index ⸻ 191

including Zombies from History in Colour! ⸻ *after p. 128*

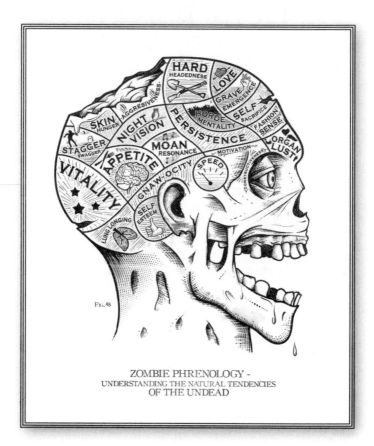

Fig. 48

ZOMBIE PHRENOLOGY -
UNDERSTANDING THE NATURAL TENDENCIES
OF THE UNDEAD

INTRODUCTION

'That rather terrible thing which there is in every photograph: the return of the dead.'

Roland Barthes, *Camera Lucinda* (2000)

'Power is possible only if death is no longer free; only if the dead are put under surveillance.'

Jean Baudrillard, *Symbolic Exchange and Death* (2000)

The Walking Dead. Walkers. Biters. Eaters. The Infected. The Contaminated. The Re-animated. Revenants. The Living Dead. Whatever you want to call them, the zombie apocalypse is coming. You know it, I know it.

So, faced with the inevitable, what do you do? Do you wait until that dull bloke from No.37 is lurching through the French windows? Or do you step up, take some pride in your actions, and take out some of history's big guns before you are finally eaten? If the latter, then you are in the right place. For, nestled within these pages, are the secrets of sixty high-value targets from Britain's illustrious (and ignoble) past. The good and the great mix with famous criminals, rebels and pirates. Do you itch to take on one of the grandees of nineteenth-century literature, or test yourself against an axe-wielding medieval bampot? Wrestle with Nelson? Battle with Boudica? Then here, friend, is your opportunity. Where they are buried, what wounds and weaknesses they bear, height, age, difficulty level – everything the fully prepared and thoughtful zombie hunter needs to know.

Other considerations will of course preoccupy you. Where will you have the maximum effect, for instance? The obvious answer would be Westminster Abbey, as eleven of our sixty notables are buried there. Thus, should your chosen target refuse to re-animate for some reason – possibly because they can't find their head – then you have a multiple choice of consolation prizes. Both Canterbury Cathedral and Winchester boast three of our distinguished dead, while London's Kensal Green Cemetery has two, as does Windsor Castle (Henry VIII and Queen Victoria) and St Paul's Cathedral (and what two – Wellington and Nelson). The others are scattered the length and breadth of these isles – although, sadly, some graves remain merely speculative to this day. Such is the nature of the ancient dead. At the very least, the zombie apocalypse should solve a whole series of historical conundrums, including the final resting places of such notables as Macbeth, Wat Tyler, Owain Glyndwr or Oliver Cromwell, not to mention a certain Jack, nicknamed the Ripper.

Contemporary zombie culture did not start with *Night of the Living Dead*. The dead have been returning for centuries. This book is peppered with accounts of those who were declared dead but yet lived; those who survived the hangman's noose or were buried alive; and descriptions of bog bodies, preserved corpses and mummified remains. Should you wish to install yourself in a defensive position, you will also find a guide to the best castles in Britain for that purpose. In addition, there are juicy bits of folklore, tall tales and unlikely legends concerning the walking dead, most taken from contemporary accounts that stretch back more than 1,000 years.

Warning: due to a lack of time, resources and inclination, no Health and Safety Reports or Statutory Risk Assessments have been produced for any of the sixty encounters outlined here. Ancient remains should be considered a biohazard, and may act as vectors for disease-carrying bacteria, insects and worms. Barrier protection and filter masks are recommended at all times, not to mention a strong stomach. Proceed at your own risk. In addition, the publishers cannot be held responsible if, having followed the advice in this book, you still end up being killed and eaten.

'An apocalypse isn't meant to be polite.'

Tony Wilson (1977)

'The control of corpses is always simultaneously about the social production of life; this is the underlying dualism that continues to haunt us so provocatively and which sustains these kinds of interrogations of the newly dead, of corpses, of our humanity and animality, the sacred and the secular, the humane and the hereafter, disgust and the erotic, sovereignty and power ... Corpses do matter.'

Deborah Posel & Pamila Gupta, *The Life of the Corpse* (2009)

ANTI-ZOMBIE WEAPONS

It may seem obvious, but it's worth remembering that zombies are not like you or me, especially when it comes to pain. They don't pay attention to mere flesh wounds. Damage to a major limb or organ will stop you in your tracks; to the shuffling undead, it's just an inconvenience. What you're looking for, then, is something that can cause maximum trauma to the zombies' Achilles heel: the neck and head area. Yes, I know in the movies and games the small packs of surviving humans take out the zombie hordes with everything from automatic weapons and grenades to flamethrowers and RPGs, but you have to ask yourself: (a) how are you going to get hold of such armaments, and (b) would you know how to use them anyway? In real life, head-shooting a moving target is not an easily acquired skill. A much more realistic scenario is that you defend yourself with whatever weapons you can scrounge or improvise. A good place to start, therefore, would be your local castle or museum, where they may well have an armoury stuffed with the kind of sharp pointy things that will be of utility to your cause. Zombies beware: we're going to get medieval on your derrière.

Pole Weapons
Forget daggers and knives: you require something with leverage, that is, a blade at the end of a long handle, so that the momentum of the swing adds to the cutting power of the blade. Look for pole arms such as:

Halberd: an axe-blade, hook and spike at the end of a 6ft-long pole. Its kissing cousin, the pollaxe, has a smaller axe or hammerhead.
Glaive: similar to a halberd, but with just a single-edged cutting

blade. Not as effective as its cousin the *voulge*, which has a more 'meat cleaver' appearance, ideal for hacking and chopping.

Bill or billhook: where the cutting blade is long and curved.

Lochaber axe: a type of Scottish halberd, with a long scythe-like blade.

Advantages: they keep the zombies 6ft away from you. And they're excellent for neck severing.

Disadvantages: all require a two-handed swing, so you can't otherwise defend yourself. Plus the effort required is very tiring.

ANTI-ZOMBIE RATING: between 😁😁😁 and 😁😁😁😁😁.

Axes, Maces and Mauls

Generally, these weapons have shorter hafts than pole weapons, so while they are easier to smash and bash with, you have to get in closer, thus risking close-combat wounds (not to mention stinking zombie-breath). Mauls are essentially war-hammers, while maces are little more than clubs – for maximum damage, seek out maces with metal ridges, spikes or flanges. Battle-axes, however, are the business: you can split a zombie skull in one blow.

ANTI-ZOMBIE RATING: maces and mauls: 😁😁; battle-axes: 😁😁😁.

Swords

Not as effective as you might think, being designed for slashing and stabbing rather than chopping and decapitation. One exception: the Samurai sword, where the quality and sharpness of the steel is so great that – with sufficient power put into your two-handed swing – you could cut a zombie in half.

ANTI-ZOMBIE RATING: swords in general: 😁; Samurai sword: 😁😁😁😁.

Bows

If you're not already a skilled archer, the zombaclypse is probably not the time to take up the bow, as it's the very devil to learn to use accurately, especially if your target is the head, the hardest part of the body to aim for. The same applies to crossbows, which are a shorter-range weapon (but with extra punch). A crossbow bolt to the chest is not a zombie-killer, however, and by the time you've slowly reloaded your weapon, well, let's just say you might have more problems than just an awkward winding mechanism. N.B.: all medieval bows in collections are too fragile to be any use, so don't bother.

ANTI-ZOMBIE RATING: 0 (unless you have a modern sports bow, and you know how to use it, in which case 💀 or 💀💀).

The New-Fangled Alternative

You could, of course, simply pop along to your nearest DIY barn, where there will be a selection of wood-splitting axes complete with lightweight but sturdy fibreglass handles, soft grips and steel heads. All will make for fine two-handled weapons, although sadly B&Q don't seem to stock the modern equivalent of voulges or halberds. A chainsaw could come in handy, although you're going to be up close and personal before you can use it (remember also to read the instructions and keep your hands behind the guard). Another good place would be the kind of family ironmongery business or traditional agricultural suppliers that are, sadly, increasingly hard to find these days. Should you locate such a gem, it will supply you with a veritable cornucopia of improvised anti-personnel devices. Rivet a razor-sharp scythe blade to a long pole, for example, and you're laughing.

ANTI-ZOMBIE RATING: between 💀 and 💀💀💀💀💀, depending on whether items are in stock ('we're expecting a delivery on Tuesday...'); quality; and your own ingenuity. N.B.: don't bother with the extended warranty.

DEFENDING THE BODY

Zombies want to sink their teeth into you; it therefore makes sense to protect your skin.

Full-body metal armour
Advantages: excellent barrier protection.
Disadvantages: (a) it's heavy and awkward; (b) helms with the visor down have very little visibility; (c) if you fall over, you're not getting up again.
ANTI-ZOMBIE RATING: 😵😵

Motorcycle clothing
Advantages: much of today's high-end anti-abrasion motorcycle clothing is reinforced with polyurethane armour at the elbows, knees, shoulders and shins, and some have stretched Kevlar fabric. Add a solid helmet and you're temporarily zombie-proof.
Disadvantages: hot and sweaty. But what do you want to be: stinky, or dead?
ANTI-ZOMBIE RATING: 😵😵😵

I'd say that the ideal would be a combination of motorbike gear, voulge, Samurai sword and hardware-store axe. Plus, you will look way cool.

And finally: a few useful locations for gathering your anti-zombie arms and armour
Belvoir Castle, Leicestershire
The British Museum (especially for Samurai swords)
Culzean Castle, Ayrshire

Inverarary Castle, Argyll
Royal Armouries Museum, Leeds
The Tower of London
The Wallace Collection, London
Warwick Castle
Windsor Castle
York Castle Museum

A Hunter's Guide

ZOMBIES
FROM HISTORY

BOUDICA,
QUEEN OF THE ICENI

AD ?—60/61

Height: A Roman writer who lived long after Boudica's time described her as 'very tall'. There are no eyewitness accounts of her true appearance.

Age at death: Unknown, but she had two daughters who were in their teens at least.

Special skills: Fury, vengeance, mass destruction and slaughter. After her husband's death, her daughters were publicly raped and she was whipped. In retaliation, Queen Boudica marshalled up to 100,000 members of the Iceni and their neighbouring tribe, the Trinovantes, and annihilated the Roman cities of Colchester and London, leaving behind a layer of burnt ash so extensive it is still known to archaeologists as 'the Boudica deposit'. The tribes also cut a legion to pieces near Cambridge, and attacked St Albans, home of the Iceni's hated neighbours the Catuvellauni – an act not of war but of ethnic cleansing.

What killed her? The over-confident Celtic army made the mistake of taking on the Romans in open battle: perhaps 80,000 Britons died, the greatest one-day slaughter until the First World War. One source says Boudica committed suicide, another that she sickened and died. Much more likely is that she was one of the piles of nameless dead.

Where is she buried? Well she's *not* buried between platforms 9 and 10 at King's Cross Station, as that is a modern myth. No-one even knows where the final battle took place. Leading candidates include Atherstone (Warwickshire), and Paulerspury or Church Stowe (both Northamptonshire). The best chance, I suggest,

would be to team up with other zombie hunters and stake out each site. With luck, one of you will encounter *thousands* of hacked-off Celtic warriors.

Weaknesses and wounds: Most of the Britons were killed with javelins or short stabbing swords, so she may be in a bad way.

Extra facts and zombie quotes: Bad-ass Boudica was responsible for ending anywhere up to 70,000 Roman lives.

Difficulty rating:

Historical disclaimer: If Boudica died in the battle there was probably no burial, as the standard rite at the time was excarnation – the bodies lying exposed to the elements and birds until only the bones were left to be scattered elsewhere. So maybe there is no body to reanimate.

the return of the dead:

ANCIENT REVENANTS?

Archaeologists have uncovered many burials from the Romano-British and Anglo-Saxon periods (fifth to eleventh centuries) in which the corpse has been treated unusually. Known as 'deviant burials', examples include decapitation (often with the skull placed at the feet or between the legs); prone (laid face down); bound, or pinned down under heavy stones. It is of course difficult to reconstruct the beliefs of the ancient people who did this to the bodies. Probably many of the burials were of the 'despised' – criminals or captured enemies – and this was a way of dishonouring the dead. This is likely when we look at heads that had been cut off from behind – the typical arrangement in a beheading execution. But many of the heads had been removed not only after death, when the blood had stopped pumping, but also from the front, with great care taken to work through the vertebrae.

The other likely possibility is that some of these rituals were designed to prevent the dead from physically returning. An elderly woman in a Romano-British burial at Guilden Morden, Cambridgeshire, had her coffin opened after death, her body partially burned in the grave, and her head cut off and placed at her feet. In a very old legend from County Derry, the evil tyrant Abhartach is buried standing up, as befits a chieftain. However, being a dread magician, he rises from his grave. Having been 'killed' and buried again, he once more quits his grave to menace the locals. This time, however, he is despatched with a sword, and then buried upside down, which seals his fate and he is never seen again above ground. Abhartach is usually described as a dwarf; it may be significant that some of the skeletons in the 'deviant burials' showed signs of physical disfigurement or disability, factors which in life may have marked them as 'uncanny'. To give but one example: in a late Roman cemetery in Poundbury, Dorset, a child who had been born deaf was buried face down.

Anglo-Saxon pagan beliefs about the abilities of the dead continued long after England had been notionally Christianized. In the 990s Christian priests were specifically banned from conducting rituals to make corpses speak and reveal secrets of the future or the location of buried treasure. This sin of necromancy was still being forbidden in the eleventh century, which shows it remained in practice.

Above all, there is a fear that the body will literally walk after death. A man left face down in an Anglo-Saxon cemetery in Cambridge had had his feet cut off after death but before burial. These deeply held notions retained their grip for centuries, and in some parts of neighbouring Lincolnshire it was commonplace in the nineteenth century to tie the toes of a corpse together. The belief in prone burials for potentially dangerous individuals – the idea being that if the corpse did re-animate, it would only burrow further into the earth – persisted even longer. As late as the First World War there was an example of British troops burying a German soldier face down in the Flanders mud.

ST PATRICK,
PATRON SAINT OF IRELAND
?—493. MAYBE.

Height: Unknown. Patrick is probably the most famous person in Irish history, yet he is utterly obscure. Most of the things many people think they 'know' about him are later traditions. Or, to put it another way, they're made up.

Age at death: Unknown.

Special skills: What skills do you need to convert a hostile nation of pagans? Perhaps a personality with a bit of grit, not to mention the ability to outfox, browbeat and co-opt a cluster of local Dark Age warlords.

What killed him? Unknown.

Where is he buried? That absolutely reliable source – tradition – says Patrick died at or near Saul, on the coast of County Down, where an enormous statue of him now stands. The remains were then allegedly interred at the site of what is now Down Cathedral in Downpatrick. In the twelfth century a freebooter named John de Courcy undertook his own Norman Conquest of Ulster, and 'miraculously' located the bones of the saint. The site swiftly became a destination for pilgrims, which was handy for anyone interested in increasing their personal revenue stream; such as, say, the local Norman landowner. De Courcy's reliability can be judged by his claim that he had also installed at Downpatrick the bones of Ireland's two other great saints, St Brigid (died perhaps around AD 524) and St Columba (died AD 597). Three for one! The pilgrims must have loved that. A large stone in the grounds of Down Cathedral, inscribed with the word 'Patric', was only installed in 1900.

Weaknesses and wounds: Unknown.

Extra facts and zombie quotes: St Patrick supposedly banished snakes from Ireland. So if you want to flush the herpeto-phobe holy man out, it might be worth taking a grass snake or two with you. (N.B. It's probably not a good idea to use adders.)

Difficulty rating:

Historical disclaimer: It seems unlikely that Downpatrick holds the bodies of three saints, or even just of Patrick. However, if by any chance a trio of Dark Age icons do emerge from the ground, all carrying giant staves, don't call us to complain – we'll be too busy fending off our own historical anomalies.

KING ARTHUR,
BRITISH LEGEND

?~?

Height: Unknown.

Age at death: Unknown.

Special skills: If there ever was an Arthur – which is not certain – then he was a fighting man and a leader. The earliest account, written in the ninth century, calls Arthur *dux bellorum* (war commander) and states that he fought twelve battles against the Saxons and others in the sixth century. Arthur may not even have been a king, just a local warlord or chieftain. Then again, nobody really knows.

What killed him? He probably died in an obscure skirmish, but one of the more popular legends tells how Arthur fought and killed his bitter incest-derived son Mordred, only to be fatally wounded himself. The final battle is often said to have been at Camlann, wherever *that* is (there are at least a dozen candidates).

Where is he buried? Well, the monks of Glastonbury claimed to have located his body within their abbey in the twelfth century, but that was just a bit of local flim-flam with an eye to pilgrims' purses. Several locations in England, Wales and Scotland all claim to be his true burial place. The orthodox view is that, having returned Excalibur to some kind of water goddess, Arthur was taken by barge to the Isle of Avalon, a mystical paradise where his wounds were healed, and from where he will return at the time of England's greatest crisis. And if a zombie apocalypse isn't a crisis, I don't know what is.

Weaknesses and wounds: The Avalon version of his fate clearly implies he will return in tip-top form.

Extra facts and zombie quotes: Arthur is already a zombie-in-waiting, as he's been in suspended Avalonian animation for 1,500 years.

Difficulty rating: 👁️👁️👁️

Historical disclaimer: If you're lucky enough to find the right grave, then beware. Arthur's game plan may go like this: recover Excalibur from its watery lock-up, gather some of the lads from the old Round Table, get Merlin and Lancelot on the team – and then, in the Dark Ages manner, embark on a campaign of mass slaughter.

the return of the dead:

THE MUMMIES OF CLADH HALLAN (c. 1100 bc)

Someone in Bronze Age Britain was making mummies. Three bodies found in 2004 at Cladh Hallan, on South Uist in the Western Isles, had been disembowelled (to prevent decay) and then deliberately preserved, possibly by being smoked, pickled or placed in a peat bog. This retained the soft tissue, and at least two of the bodies were kept above ground for about 100 years before they were finally buried as a 'foundation deposit' beneath the floor of a newly constructed roundhouse. Clearly, the revered ancestral dead were intended to watch over and protect the living. One of the bodies was actually composed of three different individuals, meaning the articulated and mummified original corpse had been 'improved' with the addition of bones from other people.

So, a small number of very important individuals had been deliberately preserved and kept available for consultation for a century, before being finally installed as the guardians of a major building. Mummies beneath the floorboards: Gothic zombie heaven.

the return of the dead:

SAINTS ORAN AND DRYTHELM
(SEVENTH CENTURY)

'A certain person, who had been some time dead, rose again to life, and related many remarkable things he had seen.' So wrote the Venerable Bede in his seventh-century masterwork *Ecclesiastical History*. The individual concerned was St Drythelm, from Northumbria:

> He died in the beginning of the night; but in the morning early, he suddenly came to life again, and sat up, upon which all those that sat about the body weeping, fled away in a great fright, only his wife, who loved him best, though in a great consternation and trembling, remained with him. He, comforting her, said, 'Fear not, for I am now truly risen from death, and permitted again to live among men; however, I am not to live hereafter as I was wont, but from henceforward after a very different manner.'

He spent the rest of his life as a hermit in the monastery of Melrose.

Drythelm related his journey in the Afterlife in terms consistent with Christian piety. In contrast, St Oran, who was (for some reason) buried alive on the Isle of Iona, and dug up again after three days, had a dissenting view. Oran exclaimed, 'There is no such great wonder in death, nor is Hell what it has been described.' At this heretical utterance, the great St Columba ordered Oran to be immediately covered with earth again, 'lest he gossip further.' It has to be said that this tale was only written down a full 300 years after it is meant to have occurred, and is almost certainly a garbled pagan version of the resurrection of Christ. Nevertheless Reilig Odhráin, Oran's Graveyard, still stands today next to Iona Abbey.

ALFRED THE GREAT,
KING OF THE ANGLO-SAXONS

849–899

Height: 5ft 8ins.

Age at death: About 50.

Special skills: Anyone who can take on the Vikings in both guerrilla warfare and open battle is a warrior to be reckoned with. Keen on education, religion, law-making and the arts, Alfred was also a brilliant strategist and military commander.

What killed him? Unknown; throughout his life he suffered from a debilitating inflammatory bowel condition, possibly Crohn's disease, but this is rarely fatal – though it is unlikely to improve his temper.

Where is he buried? Winchester, the capital of Wessex; his remains were moved and reburied at least twice in the Middle Ages, and were then lost.

Weaknesses and wounds: Alfred was the only Anglo-Saxon leader to resist the Viking blitzkrieg; a war veteran from the age of 16, he fought numerous battles, waged a guerrilla campaign from the wetlands of the Somerset marshes, turned near-defeat into victory, re-conquered half of the country, forced the Vikings into a *real-politik* compromise, created a modern army, hunted continuously, wrote books, forged stable military alliances with neighbouring kingdoms and founded the very concept of England. Er, what weaknesses?

Extra facts and zombie quotes: Alfred was a classic iron fist in a velvet glove, promoting intellectual and cultural life while being adept at killing large numbers when the situation demanded.

At the Battle of Edington in Wiltshire, 'Alfred attacked the whole pagan [Viking] army fighting ferociously in dense order, and by divine will eventually won the victory, [and] made great slaughter among them.'

Difficulty rating:

Historical disclaimer: In 2013 bones were exhumed from an unmarked grave in St Bartholomew's burial ground, awaiting analysis to see if they are Alfred's. You may have to hang round a Winchester warehouse for some time to see whether you've found your man – but if it is him, then he'll probably attack from your blind spot, kill you and your friends, and then start giving orders to any walking dead able to lift a sword. Within days, his zombie partisans will be marching on London.

AN ANGLO-SAXON VISION OF THE RESURRECTION OF THE DEAD

According to Ælfric's *Lives of the Saints*, AD 997:

> Each man yet shall have his own height in the size that he was before as a man, or that he should have had had he become fully-grown, those who departed in childhood or adolescence. Just as God shaped in soul and body, both male and female, and created them human … so he also at Doomsday raises them from the dead, both males and females, and they dwell ever so without any lust either good or evil, and no man after will ever take a wife, nor any woman take a husband, nor shall they beget children.

> Nor shall the holy ones in heaven have any blemish or ill-health, or be one-eyed, although he was before lame in his life, but his limbs shall be all sound to him, in shining brightness, and tangible in his spiritual body.

So all those zombies you were relying on to be a bit of a soft target? Not going to happen, sunshine…

the return of the dead:

ST EDMUND (AD 870)

Edmund was an obscure Christian Saxon king who resisted the Viking invasion in East Anglia. According to a hagiography written more than 100 years after his death, he was tied to a tree, beaten, peppered with arrows, and finally beheaded. The head was later recovered and buried with the body around the year 870. Between 942 and 951 Theodred, Bishop of London, found that the corpse was (a) uncorrupted, (b) free of all traces of the arrow wounds, and (c) bearing a thin scarlet line on the neck where the head had miraculously re-attached itself. Pilgrims and the sick flocked to the new shrine, now residing in the abbey at Bury St Edmunds.

About 100 years after Theodred's inspection, Leofstan, the slightly sceptical abbot at Bury St Edmunds, decided to check if the head had indeed re-attached. He had the body exhumed and, while one monk held the feet, Leofstan gave the head a good pull: it was, however, as firmly attached as in life. The body was last examined in 1198, when it was found to be entire and supple.

The improbable folklore of St Edmund may actually disguise another form of bodily preservation: there is a good chance that the alleged incorrupt remains of the saint were in fact a prehistoric bog body that had been accidentally dug up in the fens and peat bogs of East Anglia. Incorporating the preserved body into the legend of St Edmund was a brilliant idea, creating a focus for the money-spinning cult that grew up around the martyr king. The line around the neck may correspond to the garrotte which has been found on similar human sacrifices, such as Lindow Man, now in the British Museum. Sadly, Edmund's incorrupt corpse – or its bog-body substitute – was probably lost during the Reformation.

CNUT,
VIKING KING OF ENGLAND
c. 990–1035

Height: A description written long after his death says he was 'exceptionally tall and strong'.

Age at death: About 45.

Special skills: War and peace. In the early years of the eleventh century the Viking Mafia were no longer content with smash-and-grab raids, or being bribed with vast amounts of cash to keep away from England: now they wanted the entire kingdom. The Danish Conquest saw Cnut smash an English army at Ashingdon in Essex in 1016; when he became undisputed king two years later, Cnut acted in typical fashion for the times, slaughtering all the family of the deposed monarchy of Aethelred the Unready and Edmund Ironside. During an earlier incursion, Cnut had savagely mutilated English hostages delivered against Aethelred's good behaviour. Anglo-Saxon England, however, was the most efficiently governed, administered and taxed country in western Europe; Cnut therefore kept both the Church and the Dark Age civil service on his side, and ruled rather well, bringing peace and law to a war-weary nation. Cnut sometimes used English troops when he later expanded his empire into Denmark, Norway and southern Sweden.

What killed him? We have no idea.

Where is he buried? Cnut was first buried in the Old Minster at Winchester. Then his remains, along with those of the other illustrious dead, were transferred to the new, grander Winchester Cathedral in the twelfth century. During the Civil War, Roundhead ruffians scattered skeletons across the floor. Some years later the

remains were somewhat indiscriminatingly gathered up into several mortuary chests. Archaeologists are currently examining some of the bones to see if DNA comparisons with Cnut's relatives elsewhere can help identify which are his bones.

Weaknesses and wounds: We have no idea.

Extra facts and zombie quotes: Which name to use: Canute, Cnut, Knut or Knutr? Well, you could ask him, I suppose, but then he might be more interested in other matters. Like killing and eating you.

Difficulty rating:

the return of the dead:

HAROLD HAREFOOT (1040)

Harold, one of Cnut's sons, was declared King Harold I, despite the opposition of the named heir, his half-brother Hardecnut (who was conveniently away, having a few problems in Denmark at the time). When Harold died and was buried in Westminster Abbey, Hardecnut had the body exhumed, put on trial, beheaded, and thrown into the Thames. The body may have been subsequently recovered and interred in a London cemetery; a contradictory report says he ended up at Winchester.

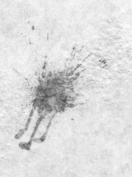

the return of the dead:

THE DRAKELOW DUO
(EARLY TWELFTH CENTURY)

Geoffrey, the abbot of Burton-on-Trent, included a brief zombiform story in his *Life and Miracles of Saint Modwenna*, written between 1118 and 1150. Two peasants were involved in a dispute between the abbey and a local lord. When they dropped dead while eating lunch – an event ascribed to the powers of St Modwenna – they were buried in their native village of Stapenhill. That very evening the pair were seen walking along the road to Drakelow village, carrying their coffins on their backs. After spending days banging on doors and shouting at the locals, the walking dead brought a plague that killed most of the inhabitants. The pestilence only ceased when the head of each corpse was hacked off and placed between their legs, their hearts torn out and burnt, and the remains reburied into nailed-shut coffins (which eerily echoes the treatment meted out to the Romano-British corpse at Guilden Morden – see p. 18). The Derbyshire village of Drakelow, which still exists, was reportedly abandoned for a long time thereafter.

In a similar tale, taken from Walter Map's *De Nugis Curialium* ('Courtier's Trifles'), written sometime before 1190, we hear of a revenant wandering the streets of Hereford, calling out the names of people who later died of disease. The remedy, prescribed by a bishop, was a combination of holy water and partial decapitation with a spade: neither was effective, however, and in the end Sir William Landon cornered the creature as it returned to its grave and spilt its head apart with his sword.

MACBETH,
KING OF SCOTS

?–1057

Height: The only contemporary account describes him as 'tall'.

Age at death: Possibly about 52.

Special skills: Warfare, close combat, and plotting. But forget everything you think you know about Macbeth. Shakespeare's play is a fantasy, based on false propagandist historical accounts. Macbeth was a hereditary *mormaer* or regional lord of Moray, at a time when most Scottish nobles perished at the hands of their power-hungry relatives. Macbeth got the job by killing his cousins (who themselves had murdered his father). Another power struggle developed when Duncan I – who, in contrast to his aged portrayal by Shakespeare, was only in his thirties – became king of the Scots. Macbeth killed him in a skirmish. King Macbeth went on to reign for seventeen years, feeling so secure as to go on pilgrimage to Rome, the only Scottish king to do so.

What killed him? Duncan's son Malcolm invaded with an Anglo-Danish force from Northumbria, supported by King Edmund of England. After three years of resistance, Macbeth died in open battle at Lumphanan in Aberdeenshire (no 'Birnam Wood came to Dunsinane', I'm afraid).

Where is he buried? The only semi-reliable account states he was buried on the holy island of Iona. But was Macbeth instead just one of the naked corpses thrown into a pit somewhere near Lumphanan?

Weaknesses and wounds: It was traditional at that time for the bodies of the significant dead to be mutilated, so he may be in a bad way.

Extra facts and zombie quotes: I am in blood / Stepp'd in so far, that, should I wade no more, / Returning were as tedious as go o'er. (William Shakespeare, *Macbeth*)

Difficulty rating: 👹👹

Historical disclaimer: I suggest heading for Iona. Not only is it an agreeable place to sit out the zombie apocalypse, but even if you don't get Macbeth you'll be assured of some action as scores of Scotland's early gangster-kings struggle up out of the ground.

WILLIAM I,
THE CONQUEROR
c. 1029–1087

Height: 5ft 10ins – and burly to boot.

Age at death: Probably 59.

Special skills: War. William inherited the Duchy of Normandy when still a child, and an illegitimate one at that. Not surprisingly, he saw massed corpses from an early age, and grew up cold-blooded and merciless. The Norman Conquest was just one episode in a lifetime of riding into battle and laying waste to all around him. He was the original hard bastard.

What killed him? He suddenly became extraordinarily fat, which suggests he might have had a condition of the bowel or stomach. Whilst surveying the burning of yet another French town, William's horse reared and the point of his saddle, driven into the grotesque weight of the king's body, penetrated either his lower abdomen or his perineum. William took another ten days to die of his internal injuries.

Where is he buried? The moment the king expired, chaos erupted. Everyone present at the deathbed in Rouen either trousered as much portable loot as possible, or hid from the expected meltdown of law and order. William's naked body was left unattended until a minor knight was persuaded to take it by river to Caen. There the huge corpse, bloated further by the gases of decomposition, would not fit in the coffin and burst, filling the church with the worst of all smells.

Weaknesses and wounds: William survived a lifetime of mayhem with few wounds, only slowing down with his final ballooning illness.

Extra facts and zombie quotes: You're obviously going to need a daytrip to France for this one, assuming the ferries continue to run during the zombie apocalypse (N.B. duty free may not be available). Alternatively, if total breakdown of society occurs, why not borrow a helicopter from one of the army bases in the south of England and hop across the Channel? You know, like in the movies.

Difficulty rating: 👓👓👓👓

Historical disclaimer: The tomb at Caen was destroyed in the sixteenth century and the remains scattered. In 1987 the French authorities announced they had rediscovered William's remaining thighbone. Is it worth the trip? Well, it is William the flippin' Conqueror...

WILLIAM RUFUS,
KING OF ENGLAND

c. 1056–1100

Height: 'Not very tall', according to a chronicler, but possessing 'astonishing strength'.

Age at death: About 44.

Special skills: Upper-class thuggery. Rufus ('the red-faced') was one of several sons of William the Conqueror. He was a nasty piece of work, inheriting his father's fighting abilities and casual cruelty, without any of the concomitant political *nous*. Although he was good at killing the Scots, Welsh, French and rebellious Norman barons, William was never popular and alienated large parts of his kingdom.

What killed him? The simple answer is a crossbow bolt to the chest, while he was hunting in the New Forest. But then you have the medieval conspiracy theory. Was it an accident, a simple misplaced shot from one of his hunting companions? Or is it significant that William's younger brother Henry just happened to be nearby, within a quick gallop of Winchester, where he seized the Royal Treasury in an undignified bank raid and quickly had himself proclaimed king? William Rufus is the medieval JFK.

Where is he buried? The body of the king lay in a woodland glade, either where it fell (by accident) or was carefully placed (by the putative assassins). It was found by some rustics, who conveyed it to Winchester Cathedral on a wagon, the corpse bleeding copiously all the way. The funeral was brief, the courtiers having found something more interesting to do – sucking up to the new king, Henry I.

Weaknesses and wounds: Some minor wounds aside, William seems to have been in good health. Apart from that bolt out of the blue, of course.

Extra facts and zombie quotes: According to one source, the clerics at Winchester refused to grant the wicked king post-mortem absolution for his sins, and, further, no prayers or masses were said for his soul. According to the belief at the time, then, Rufus went straight to hell. One suspects he won't be a happy camper.

Difficulty rating: 🎃🎃🎃

Historical disclaimer: As with Cnut, his grave at Winchester has been moved and rifled, and his bones may be mixed up in the several mortuary chests on display. Or they may not. But he is somewhere in the cathedral. Probably.

THOMAS BECKET,
ARCHBISHOP
c. 1118–1170

Height: About 6ft.

Age at death: About 52.

Special skills: Obstreperousness. Becket was a smart lad, a London merchant's son who moved up the ladder of Church administration until his obvious skills landed him the plum job of Lord Chancellor to Henry II. When he became Archbishop of Canterbury, however, Becket had a spiritual crisis, embraced asceticism and opposed Henry's power-grab of the Church's privileges. Standing up to the ruthless Plantagenet king took some doing. The staring contest between the two former best friends lasted for years, a struggle of wills that could only end in blood.

What killed him? Eventually, Henry lost patience. Four of his knights committed the famous 'murder in the cathedral'.

Where is he buried? Canterbury Cathedral, although his shrine was destroyed during the Dissolution of the Monasteries and his bones scattered. The skull, however, may still be beneath the Corona (or 'Becket's Crown') at the east end of the cathedral.

Weaknesses and wounds: One knight sliced through the top of the skull, the second severed the head at the neck, and the third scooped out the brains and spread them over the floor, saying, 'Let us away, knights; this fellow will arise no more.' Well, until...

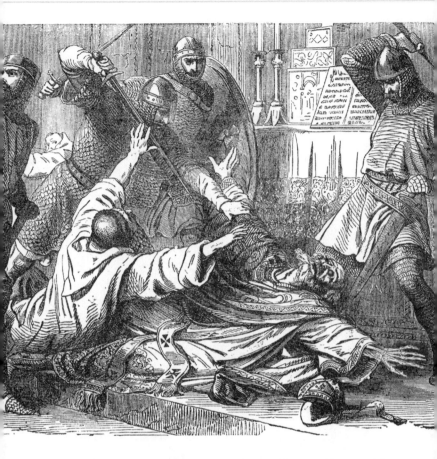

Extra facts and zombie quotes: The Bishop of Exeter said of Becket, 'Truly he is dead, but his power lives on.' Should Cockney Tom actually re-animate, do take time to shout out, 'Will no-one rid me of this turbulent priest?' before doing the job yourself.

Difficulty rating:

the return of the dead:

THE MAN FROM ANANTIS
(LATE TWELFTH CENTURY)

A 'man of evil conduct' fled from York to the castle of Anantis, where he subsequently died in a fall. After the burial his corpse 'wandered through the courts and around the houses while all men made fast their doors… for fear of meeting and being beaten black and blue by this vagrant monster.' The revenant's presence brought an epidemic which killed many and emptied the village. Two young men dug up the corpse, and:

> …dragging it beyond the village, they speedily constructed a funeral pile; and upon one of them saying that the pestilential body would not burn unless its heart were torn out, the other laid open its side by repeated blows of the blunted spade, and, thrusting in his hand, dragged out the accursed heart. This being torn piecemeal, and the body now consigned to the flames … When that infernal hell-hound had thus been destroyed, the pestilence which was rife among the people ceased, as if the air, which had been corrupted by the contagious motions of the dreadful corpse, were already purified by the fire which had consumed it.

The episode is in *Historia Rerum Anglicarum* (*The History of the Affairs of England*), written in about 1198 by the chronicler William of Newburgh, who says he was told it by a monk who was an eyewitness to the events in his youth. 'Anantis' is unknown to us, although it may mean Alnwick in Northumberland, or Annan or Anand in Scotland.

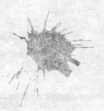

William's history – largely a chronicle of the reigns of Stephen, Henry II and Richard I – is a minor treasure trove of such zombie stories. We read, for example, 'of the prodigy of the dead man, who wandered about after burial.' This deceased gentleman from Buckinghamshire, 'having entered the bed where his wife was reposing, he not only terrified her on awaking, but nearly crushed her by the insupportable weight of his body.' He returned for another two nights, but, having been repulsed, moved on to harass his brothers, 'but being repelled by the carefulness and valour of the watchers, he rioted among the animals, both indoors and outdoors.' The venerable Bishop Hugh of Lincoln laid the revenant by having a letter of absolution (a pardon for sins) placed on the chest of the corpse: 'he was thenceforth never more seen to wander, nor permitted to inflict annoyance or terror upon any one.'

William also describes similar events at Berwick-upon-Tweed and Melrose; in both cases the walking corpse was dismembered and burned. The historian also claimed that such cases were relatively common:

> It would not be easy to believe that the corpses of the dead should sally (I know not by what agency) from their graves, and should wander about to the terror or destruction of the living… did not frequent examples, occurring in our own times, suffice to establish this fact, to the truth of which there is abundant testimony … Were I to write down all the instances of this kind which I have ascertained to have befallen in our times, the undertaking would be beyond measure laborious and troublesome.

LLEWELLYN THE GREAT,

PRINCE OF NORTH WALES

c. 1173–1240

Height: Unknown.

Age at death: Probably about 67.

Special skills: Pragmatism. Llewellyn was one of those medieval warriors who recognised that the sword wasn't enough: to hold onto power you needed to make deals. Once he had secured North Wales by (a) taking on his own family and (b) getting rid of his neighbours, Llewellyn embarked on a strategy that combined fire and slaughter with practical diplomacy. He negotiated with other Welsh princes, the papacy, the Anglo-Norman lords who controlled the Welsh lowlands and borders, the king of France, and two successive English kings (John and Henry III). Of course, once those carefully brokered alliances broke down – which they often did – Llewellyn was more than willing to go to war, and towns from Shrewsbury to Haverfordwest felt his wrath. Llewellyn was the dominant force in Wales for forty years, an astonishing feat in the snakepit of medieval politics.

What killed him? Probably a paralytic stroke.

Where is he buried? Llewellyn was buried in Aberconwy Abbey, the most important abbey in North Wales. Forty-three years after his death the abbey (and Llewellyn's bones) moved further up the Conwy valley to Maenan, the relocation taking place at the behest of Edward I, who was having a little trouble with the Welsh and wanted to build a stonking great castle on the site of the original abbey. In 1537, with the Dissolution of the Monasteries, the site at Maenan was destroyed and Llewellyn's bones lost. His massive stone sarcophagus eventually resurfaced and can be seen in the Gwydir Chapel of St Gwrst church in Llanwrst on the A470.

Weaknesses and Wounds: Unknown.

Extra facts and zombie quotes: The best-known story associated with Llewellyn concerns his hound Gelert. Llewellyn killed the dog because he thought it had fatally attacked his son, when in fact the blood on the dog's muzzle came from a marauding wolf that the faithful Gelert had just dispatched. The entire tale is sheer hokum, so don't expect any canine companions should you manage to locate Llewellyn in Llanwrst.

Difficulty rating: 👁️👁️

the return of the dead:

THE WICKED MONK (ABOUT 1296)

The not-entirely-reliable *Chronicle of Lanercost*, written in the fourteenth century, tells of a wicked monk who, long after being buried, troubled first a monastery and then the house of Sir Duncan de Insula or Delisle, some 4 miles from Paisley in the west of Scotland. The revenant's body was 'hideous, gross and tangible', and he 'savagely threw to the ground and battered those who attempted to struggle with him as nearly to shatter all their joints'. One evening at the knight's home, 'this malignant creature came in their midst, throwing them into confusion with missiles and blows', and killing Sir Duncan's son. We are not told what happened to the zombiform entity, and the anonymous author does not mention how he came by the story.

As with the stories told by Geoffrey of Burton, Walter Map and William of Newburgh, this zombie walked because he led an evil life – a common piece of medieval moralising.

WILLIAM WALLACE,
SCOTTISH PATRIOT

?–1305

Height: Accounts of Wallace's life written long after he died state that he was a giant of man, around 6ft 6ins. This may simply be wishful thinking, as we know very little about Wallace. But he was certainly taller than Mel Gibson.

Age at death: Unknown; he was probably in his mid-30s.

Special skills: Fighting and leadership. Wallace should never have been famous. He was a nobody from nowhere, and he had probably been a forest outlaw. Yet somehow he became the joint leader of a Scottish army that brilliantly overwhelmed a much larger English force at the Battle of Stirling Bridge in 1297. The upstart was quickly knighted and created Guardian of Scotland – basically Commander-in-Chief – but he was always an alien among the aristocracy. Long after most of the Scottish nobles were willing to compromise with Edward I, Wallace bloody-mindedly kept up a guerrilla campaign, utterly convinced of the rightness of his cause. Ruthless, incredibly violent, and heroically determined, Wallace had the kind of charisma that made men follow him into the very jaws of hell.

What killed him? Betrayed by his own side, Wallace was treated as a murdering low-class outlaw scumbag – which, from the English point of view, he was. A show trial in Westminster Hall was followed by the worst of all deaths – dragged head-downward through the streets by horses, hanged until not quite dead, castrated, disembowelled, the intestines burnt, the heart cut out, and then the head removed and the body butchered into four parts.

Where is he buried? The dismembered quarters were sent to Berwick, Newcastle, Perth and Stirling, where they were displayed as a warning to others. The head was placed on London Bridge. A plaque on the north wall of St Bart's Hospital, south of Smithfield Market, records the place of execution.

Weaknesses and wounds: Um, see above.

Extra facts and zombie quotes: He was never known as Braveheart. That name was given to Robert the Bruce (see p. 58).

Difficulty rating: 🎭🎭🎭 (or, alternatively, 0)

Historical disclaimer: Let's face it, there's not going to be anything left to re-animate, is there? Mind you, that Willie Wallace was one thrawn fellow...

EDWARD I,
KING OF ENGLAND

1239–1307

Height: 6ft 2ins.

Age at death: 68.

Special skills: Here's a hint: one of his nicknames was 'Hammer of the Scots', or more simply 'The Hammer'. Intimidatingly tall and tempestuous, his personality alone was enough to make more timid men fill their britches. Put a sword in his hand and you have the classic medieval killing machine, laying into rebellious barons, discontented Welshmen and independence-minded Scots with equal gusto. If you want to score maximum points, this is your target.

What killed him? After a lifetime of war, Edward ended his life being carried about in a litter. He was on his way to another campaign in Scotland when he died in Burgh by Sands in Cumbria, probably from rectal cancer.

Where is he buried? Westminster Abbey.

Weaknesses and wounds: Edward survived an attack by poisoned dagger, killing the assassin personally. Falling stones, lightning bolts, javelins and siege weapons always just missed him. Dozens of battles, leading from the front, parading in front of the walls of enemy castles, and getting stuck in with sword, lance and mace; all this, and no major wounds apart from a couple of cracked ribs: a charmed life.

Extra facts and zombie quotes: Edward supposedly made two requests on his deathbed. Firstly, that his heart should be taken to the Holy Land, accompanied by a force of 100 knights to fight the Saracens. And secondly, that his body should be boiled down so that his bones could be carried in front of his army as they took on the Scots. If these claims are true, neither were heeded. In 1774 the tomb at Westminster was opened and the body was declared intact and in 'a reasonable state of pres-ervation', so presumably it had been embalmed. The Latin inscription reads *Hic est Malleus Scottorum* – 'Here lies the Hammer of the Scots'.

Difficulty rating:

Historical disclaimer: Maybe after all these centuries, he'll have become mild-mannered, reflective, looking for the quiet life – nah, didn't think so.

EDWARD II,
KING OF ENGLAND
1284-1327

Height: 6ft.

Age at death: 43.

Special skills: Edward II wasn't really king material. For much of his reign he was only nominally in charge, and after years of anarchy, incompetence, rebellion and general mismanagement, his end came when his wife Isabella and her lover Roger Mortimer led a coup. His one special skill was intense loyalty to his friends, which was counterbalanced by his tendency to annoy the heck out of everyone else.

What killed him? Imprisoned in Berkeley Castle, Gloucestershire, Edward was pressed to the floor with a heavy door, which allowed his assailants to open his anus with a horn and thrust a red-hot spit or poker into his bowels. He took several hours to die. This appalling act had the double advantage of leaving no mark on the outside of the body, while at the same time making an obvious comment about the king's much-despised homosexuality.

Where is he buried? Significantly, Edward was not buried in Westminster Abbey, but 'out in the country', in Gloucester Cathedral, where his beautiful tomb (paid for by his son, Edward III) can still be admired.

Weaknesses and wounds: Having a red-hot iron thrust up your arse isn't exactly going to make you fighting fit; other than that, however, Edward was in good health.

Extra facts and zombie quotes: History has generally dismissed Edward as a 'weak' king, but he was ruthless when he wanted to be. And let's not forget – he was murdered on the orders of his wife and her lover, in the most homophobic manner imaginable: he is going to be one mightily pissed-off gay zombie.

Difficulty rating:

Historical disclaimer: Every 'significant' death creates its own folklore. According to rumour, Edward supposedly killed a porter and escaped from Berkeley just before the hit squad arrived. The tardy would-be assassins, fearing the wrath of the queen, promptly substituted the porter's body for that of the king. It's an unlikely tale, but if you're hanging around Gloucester Cathedral and a prole pops out of the king's tomb, don't blame me.

ANTI-ZOMBIE CASTLES

From a military point of view, zombies are effectively light infantry – deadly at close quarters and *en masse*, but with no long-range ability (such as that provided by archers or artillery). It therefore makes sense not to engage them in city streets – urban warfare is the zombie's *metier* – but in places that were originally built for defence against ravaging hordes: castles.

Now, much as you would perhaps like to imagine yourself installed as lord of the manor in some stately home, taking pot-shots at the peasants – er, sorry, zombies – as they crawl over the ha-ha, in truth a big country house built for posh balls and below-stairs rumpy with the servants is not going to be easy to defend. Too many large windows, multiple points of entry, and no easily defined killing field. No, to do the job properly, you need a hardcore, old-school, full-on medieval fortress. Ideally you want a place with a decently complete curtain wall or outer defences; a few highly defended points of entry; and a roof (it's bad enough having to take on the walking dead without being soaked through at the same time).

Here, then, are the best ten castles in which to ride out the apocalypse. All are open to the public, so you may want to visit and check them out in advance – a bit of forward planning never goes amiss when dealing with the wholesale rise of the dead from their graves and the consequent total breakdown of society.

1 THE TOWER OF LONDON (Owner: Historic Royal Palaces)
Advantages: Centrally located as a metropolitan bolt-hole; outer defences are in good shape; military garrison already on site (the Yeomen Warders); already secure (the Crown Jewels are under

guard here); two ready-to-roll siege engines on site; decent caff.
Disadvantages: Large numbers of the noble dead are buried in the Tower (see p. 73), so within the walls you'll have to contend with a zombie fifth column.
Anti-zombie rating: 💀💀💀💀

2 DOVER CASTLE, KENT (Owner: English Heritage)
Advantages: Excellent outer defences combined with strategic situation on a cliff-edge; miles of tunnels from medieval, Napoleonic and Second World War times; the Great Tower offers a superb last-ditch retreat. It took on the Nazis: it can do the same with zombies.
Disadvantages: St-Mary-in-Castro church is inside the castle. It has an old graveyard. Uh-oh…
Anti-zombie rating: 💀💀💀💀💀

3 CAERPHILLY CASTLE, CAERPHILLY (Owner: CADW)
Advantages: Second largest castle in Britain (after Windsor); siege engines on site; portcullises still in working order; impregnable water defences.
Disadvantages: We are of course assuming that zombies can't swim. Or walk underwater…
Anti-zombie rating: 💀💀💀

4 EDINBURGH CASTLE, SCOTLAND (Owner: Historic Scotland)
Advantages: Superb strategic position on a cliff-edged rock; outer walls largely in tip-top condition; strength in depth, allowing you to fall back to further defences; soldiers garrisoned in the castle; lots of swords to hand.
Disadvantages: As with the Tower of London and Dover, you've got the slight issue of multiple burials inside the castle: soldiers, traitors, criminals – and dogs.
Anti-zombie rating: 💀💀💀

5 BODIAM CASTLE, EAST SUSSEX (Owner: The National Trust)
Advantages: Completely surrounded by a titanic moat; murder holes in the gatehouse – ideal for dropping unpleasant items onto unwanted guests. It's unlikely anyone ever poured boiling oil through murder holes, but there are recorded cases of assailants

enduring heavy stones, boiling water, molten lead and heated sand. Improvise! Curtain wall and towers complete, although much of the interior is ruined; small enough to be defended by a modest band of determined survivalists.

Disadvantages: See Caerphilly Castle for potential concerns about security of aquatic defences.

Anti-zombie rating: 👁👁👁

6 CAERNARFON CASTLE, GWYNEDD (Owner: CADW)

Advantages: Complete outer walls, intimidatingly tall and 10ft thick, with thirteen towers; murder holes and portcullises; arrow slits in the towers cover every angle of approach to the walls.

Disadvantages: Some parts not fully roofed, so the accommodation might be a bit basic.

Anti-zombie rating: 👁👁👁👁

7 CARLISLE CASTLE, CUMBRIA (Owner: English Heritage)

Advantages: A proper, no-nonsense medieval fortress, used as an army base until 1959; all walls complete and standing to their full height, including the wall of the inner bailey; plenty of accommodation: you can hunker down here for the long haul; military museum on site gives handy access to weapons of different periods; principal gatehouse still has portcullis.

Disadvantages: It's not as glamorous as some of its more famous cousins. But this is the zombie apocalypse, not *Celebrity Castle.*

Anti-zombie rating: 👁👁👁👁👁

8 LEEDS CASTLE, KENT (Private owners)

Advantages: Surrounded by a major moat, with attackers from the land channelled through a single point of entry; a real posh gaff – the polar opposite of Carlisle's northern grit. This is zombie survival with style; hosted everything from the Camp David meetings to the G8 Summit – so you know the security has been sussed out; get about by ferry boat, punt and miniature train.

Disadvantages: You'll never get in: the first hint of zombie warfare and all the toffs and politicians will be heading straight for it.

Anti-zombie rating: 👁👁👁

9 WARWICK CASTLE, WARWICKSHIRE (Private owners)

Advantages: Curtain walls: check; tall towers: check; strong gatehouse: check; ballista: check: the world's largest fireball-throwing trebuchet: check; jousting area so you can charge down zombies with a lance: check.

Disadvantages: Perhaps a little too much tourist glitz and not enough opportunities for zombie slaughter? You be the judge.

Anti-zombie rating: 💀💀💀

10 EILEAN DONAN, KYLE OF LOCHALSH (Private owners)

Advantages: Small complete castle located on an island surrounded by three sea lochs. Ideal if you have a boat – or, even better, one of those Second World War amphibious DUKWs; land access by a single, easily defensible causeway; intimate and sensibly proportioned for a small number of defenders; bask in a setting made famous in dozens of films; the sparsely populated Highlands will have fewer of those pesky zombies to deal with.

Disadvantages: Bring a coat. On second thought, bring several coats. There's weather.

Anti-zombie rating: 💀💀💀💀

ROBERT THE BRUCE,
KING OF SCOTS
1274–1329

Height: 5ft 11ins, or 6ft 1in, tall for the time.

Age at death: 55.

Special skills: When you're at war you don't need a nice guy in charge; you want a psychopathic, battle-hungry beserker. Having brutally defeated his rivals for the kingship of Scotland, Bruce fought an impressive guerrilla war against the English before trouncing the forces of Edward II at the Battle of Bannockburn, during which he killed one of the premier English knights in single combat, splitting the man's head in two with a battle-axe. Bruce's victories, combined with later devastating raids into northern England, eventually led to the English recognising Scotland as an independent nation. A brilliant battlefield tactician, an inspiring leader and a terrifying warrior, Bruce was as formidable as the Middle Ages get.

What killed him? The conventional story is that he died of leprosy, but this is unlikely, although he did have a disfiguring skin condition. It may have been a series of strokes that felled the doughty warrior.

Where is he buried? Dunfermline Abbey. Sir James Douglas carried Bruce's heart into battle against the Moors in Spain. The heart and its casket were later buried in Melrose Abbey. The heart was unearthed in 1920 and again in 1996, and now lies once more at Melrose. Bruce's body was rediscovered in 1818, being reburied at Dunfermline the following year, but not before some teeth and finger bones were removed as souvenirs.

Weaknesses and wounds: Bruce appeared to have no major wounds, although a lifetime of war must have left some scars. Before his final illness Bruce was as strong as an ox.

Extra facts and zombie quotes: A modern facial reconstruction, based on a plaster-cast made during the nineteenth-century discovery, shows a boxer's face, battered by combat.

Difficulty rating:

Historical disclaimer: When the skeleton was re-interred in 1819 it was sealed in a new lead coffin with 1,500lbs of molten pitch. Even Robert the Bruce may have a bit of difficulty working his way through that.

EDWARD,
THE BLACK PRINCE
1330-1376

Height: At least 6ft.

Age at death: 45.

Special skills: Fighting, fighting and fighting. One of the key figures in the Hundred Years War, he was both ferocious in close combat and a master of battlefield tactics. To imagine just how much of a hero this handsome, charismatic warrior was to fourteenth-century England, think David Beckham crossed with Nelson – then add Hollywood-style glamour (Errol Flynn or Brad Pitt, depending on your generation). To the French he was almost some kind of demon, and one of the theories for the name 'the Black Prince' suggests it comes from *prins noire*, the man who not only humiliated them in battle but also massacred civilians with utmost brutality.

What killed him? Probably amoebic dysentery, a disease he (and much of the English army) picked up while on campaign in Spain.

Where is he buried? Canterbury Cathedral. His tomb is surmounted by an impressive gilt-bronze effigy of him in full battle armour, while replicas of his helm, gauntlets, quilted surcoat, shield and scabbard hang above (the originals are elsewhere in the cathedral, safe behind glass). His sword was stolen during the Commonwealth period – possibly, so legend states, by Oliver Cromwell himself.

Weaknesses and wounds: In his last years he became a near-invalid. However, you're looking at someone who personally killed hundreds, survived endless warfare with no serious wounds, and is pretty handy with edged weapons. Approach with extreme caution.

Extra facts and zombie quotes: The epitaph on his tomb is pure zombie poetry:

Such as thou art, sometime was I.
Such as I am, such shalt thou be.
I thought little on th'our of Death
So long as I enjoyed breath.
But now a wretched captive am I,
Deep in the ground, lo here I lie.
My beauty great, is all quite gone,
My flesh is wasted to the bone.

Difficulty rating:

WAT TYLER,
REBEL LEADER

c. 1341–1381

Height: Unknown. As with so many people from this period, we know next to nothing about Tyler, despite his role in the Peasants' Revolt (which was conspicuous for its absence of peasants).

Age at death: Around 40.

Special skills: Leading a rebellion that almost changed the course of history. Popular movements sometimes choose their own captains, and this seems to be what happened with Tyler. Battered by restrictive laws and an unfair poll tax, the yeomen, artisans and other aspirational denizens of lower-middle-class southern England became mightily disaffected. Rebellions broke out first in Essex before spreading to Kent, where the previously obscure Tyler came to prominence, presumably because his fellow rebels recognised his leadership qualities. The large rebel armies then brought fire, destruction and severed heads to London, threatening the very fabric of the government.

What killed him? With great personal courage, the 14-year-old Richard II met the rebels in person at Smithfield. Various officers of his regime had already been murdered; he might go the same way. Tyler negotiated with the king face to face. Promises were made, agreements to the rebels' demands acceded. What happened next depends on which of the many accounts you believe. Certainly a tussle between Tyler and some of the king's party took place, which resulted in Tyler being run through with a sword several times. He headed back to the rebel lines but only managed a few paces before falling from his horse. His companions took him to St Bartholomew's Hospital, from where he was abducted by the king's men, dragged back to Smithfield, and beheaded. His severed

head was displayed on a pole. Mass executions and other punitive measures re-established feudal power. All the concessions promised to the rebels were utterly forgotten.

Where is he buried? There is no record for Tyler's grave. He was probably buried in a pit near where he was killed, at Smithfield.

Weaknesses and wounds: Several stab wounds and a severed head. Not healthy.

Extra facts and zombie quotes: He may well be somewhere near William Wallace (see p. 48) – a formidable pairing of rebels, I'd wager.

Difficulty rating:

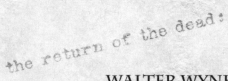
the return of the dead:

WALTER WYNKEBURN
(1363)

Henry of Knighton's *Chronicle* says that in 1363:

> One Walter Wynkeburn ... after having been taken down from the gallows
> as a dead man, was being carried to the cemetery of the Holy Sepulchre
> of Leicester, to be buried, began to revive in the cart, and was taken into
> the church of the Holy Sepulchre by an ecclesiastic, and there diligently
> guarded by this Leicester ecclesiastic to prevent his being seized for the pur-
> pose of being hanged a second time. To this man King Edward [Edward
> III] granted pardon in Leicester Abbey.

Edward is supposed to have said, 'God granted you life, so we grant
you the pardon.' In the thirteenth century Henry III had granted a
similar pardon to Judith de Balsham, who 'hanged from nine o'clock on
Monday morning, till *sun rising* on Tuesday following, and yet escaped
with life.' And we also have on record Margaret Everard of Burgh-by-
Waynflete, who was hanged at Lincoln in 1282, and revived next to the
grave intended for her. Her recovery was ascribed to a miracle, so she
was pardoned and was still alive eight years later.

> 'Such is the condition of humanity, and so uncertain is men's judgment,
> that they cannot determine even death itself.'

> Pliny

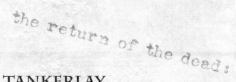

JAMES TANKERLAY
(LATE FOURTEENTH CENTURY)

Around the year 1400 an anonymous monk of Byland Abbey in Yorkshire described a series of supernatural events in the local area. Although largely thought of as 'ghost stories', in many of them the dead are clearly described as physical walking corpses. One man, Robert the Younger, 'used to come out of his grave at night and disturb and terrify the townsfolk, and all the town dogs used to follow him about, barking loudly.' This walker was pinned to the church stile by two youths, who held the corpse until the priest arrived to absolve the dead man's sins. Once this was done the undead man returned to his grave, and religious forgiveness laid the rest of the revenants in a similar manner – all except one:

> Old people tell how a certain James Tankerlay, formerly Rector of Kirkby, was buried in the Chapter House at Byland, but used to walk forth as far as Kirkby by night, and one night he struck out one eye of his former mistress. And it is said that the abbot and monks had his body dug up from the grave, together with the coffin, and forced Roger Wayneman to cart it as far as Gormire, and how when they were throwing this coffin in the water the oxen almost sank in too in their terror. May I not be in any peril myself for writing such things, for I have written just what I heard from my seniors! And may God Omnipotent have mercy on him, if indeed he might be among the number of those to be saved!

HENRY IV,
KING OF ENGLAND
1367–1413

Height: 5ft 10ins, and powerfully built.

Age at death: 46.

Special skills: (a) Usurping the throne and deposing his cousin, Richard II; (b) probably murdering Richard, perhaps through starvation or poison; (c) fighting off rebellions from, among others, Owain Glyndwr (see p. 68) and Henry 'Hotspur' Percy; (d) having not one but two plays written about him by Shakespeare.

What killed him? Some kind of epileptic attack, a long-term condition in which he suffered fits, when it was often difficult to tell – rather fittingly, given the subject of this book – whether the king was alive or dead.

Where is he buried? Beneath a beautiful alabaster monument in Canterbury Cathedral.

Weaknesses and wounds: In his later life Henry suffered an unknown disfiguring skin disease; this was widely regarded at the time as leprosy, and a punishment for his sins, but the exhumation (below) clearly shows Henry was not a leper.

Extra facts and zombie quotes: There was a rumour, circulated soon after Henry's death, that his body had actually been cast into the sea during its voyage from Westminster to Canterbury. As a result, antiquarians eventually persuaded the Dean of Canterbury to have the tomb opened. The following account appeared in *Archaeologia: or miscellaneous tracts relating to antiquity* in 1832:

To the astonishment of all present, the face of the deceased King was seen in complete preservation. The nose elevated, the cartilage even remaining, though, on the admission of the air, it sunk rapidly away, and had entirely disappeared before the examination was finished. The skin of the chin was entire, of the consistence and thickness of the upper leather of a shoe, brown and moist; the beard thick and matted, and of a deep russet colour. The jaws were perfect, and all the teeth in them, except one fore tooth, which had probably been lost during the King's life. The opening of the lead was not large enough to expose the whole of the features, and we did not examine the eyes or forehead. But the surveyor stated that when he introduced his finger under the wrappers to remove them, he distinctly felt the orbits of the eyes prominent in their sockets. The flesh upon the nose was moist, clammy, and of the same brown colour as every other part of the face.

Difficulty rating:

OWAIN GLYNDWR,
PRINCE OF WALES
1350s– c. 1416

Height: Unknown.

Age at death: 60–65.

Special skills: If you want a pat comparison, Glyndwr was the Welsh William Wallace, an unlikely rebel who rose to unexpected prominence and just wouldn't give up. An established member of the Anglo-Welsh Marcher nobility, Glyndwr had studied law in London, and had fought for Richard II in Scotland. Thereafter, comfortable obscurity would have beckoned, had not a land dispute with a fellow Marcher lord escalated out of control. In 1400 the 40-year-old Glyndwr, who seemed, to many disaffected Welsh, to embody some kind of mystical prophesised deliverance, found himself heading a full-scale revolt against Henry IV. He was declared Prince of Wales, and proved such a capable military leader that for a time much of Wales was under his control. Henry IV instituted severe punitive measures; combined with the devastation caused by the war, Wales took a generation to recover. The later years of the revolt were characterised by guerrilla warfare, with Glyndwr on the run, fighting to the bitter end. Unlike Wallace, he was never betrayed.

What killed him? No-one knows what happened to him. Like Arthur, he is the 'deathless prince' who will one day return to save Wales during its greatest crisis.

Where is he buried? The comparison with King Arthur extends to the speculation surrounding Glyndwr's resting place. Candidates include Kentchurch and Monnington Straddel on the Herefordshire/Monmouthshire border, Cwm Hir near Llandrindod,

Llanwrda near Llandovery ... and about a dozen other places. To track him down, bone up on Welsh mythography, buy a bunch of maps, and hope for the best.

Weaknesses and wounds: Unknown.

Extra facts and zombie quotes: Like Elvis, Owain Glyndwr is not dead. OK?

Difficulty rating:

HENRY VII,
KING OF ENGLAND
1457–1509

Height: 'Above the average,' which may mean he was between 5ft 7ins and 5ft 9ins.

Age at death: 52.

Special skills: Winning and making money. Since 1455 the Wars of the Roses – a dynastic battle between the houses of York and Lancaster – had bespattered England with blood, and seen off two kings, Henry VI (Lancaster) and Edward IV (York), plus several princes, dukes and earls. In 1485 the Yorkist King Richard III fell at the Battle of Bosworth, and the crown was placed on the head of an outsider from Wales – Henry Tudor, the founder of a new dynasty. For the rest of his reign Henry VII, not a fighting man, cleverly and cautiously defeated Yorkist plots and armies and promoted stability and peace, along the way building a personal fortune that he hoarded with a miser's passion.

What killed him? Tuberculosis.

Where is he buried? Westminster Abbey, with a splendid Renaissance memorial. His painted plaster death-mask, part of his effigy, is on display in the Undercroft Museum.

Weaknesses and wounds: Although he became ill and frail in later life, in his earlier days Henry had enjoyed hunting and real tennis.

Extra facts and zombie quotes: Compared to his colourful Tudor descendants, historians have generally found Henry VII a bit dull – the chartered accountant king, the money-grabbing

monarch. If he's not in the abbey when you arrive, head for the Bank of England, where the king will be in his counting-house, counting out his money.

Difficulty rating:

ANNE BOLEYN,
QUEEN CONSORT OF ENGLAND
BETWEEN 1501 AND 1509–1536

Height: Between 5ft and 5ft 3in.

Age at death: Somewhere between 28 and 35; Anne is one of the most controversial women in British history, and many of the 'facts' about her are debated, not least the actual year of her birth.

Special skills: A mysterious allure. The besotted Henry VIII annulled his marriage to Catherine of Aragon to be with Anne – and, incidentally, split with the Catholic Church of Rome in the process, turning England into a Protestant nation. Also quite good at dancing, archery, hunting – and, according to the trial records, witchcraft.

What killed her? Found guilty of 'treasonable conspiracy to procure the king's death', she was beheaded at the Tower of London. At great expense, Henry imported Jean Rombaud, a specialist executioner from Calais, for the task – as part of his job application the Frenchman severed the heads of two criminals with just one stroke of his sword. 'I heard say the executioner was very good', said Anne, laughing and putting her hands round her throat, 'and I have a little neck'. The little neck proved to be no impediment, and – in contrast to the often brutal, hacking nature of execution by axe – the sword parted Anne's head from her body in one swift action.

Where is she buried? The body was placed in a disused arrow chest and buried in an unmarked grave in the crypt of the Chapel of St Peter ad Vincula adjoining Tower Green. Nineteenth-century renovations uncovered a skeleton which was almost certainly Anne's. A modern glass memorial was unveiled in 2006, so there should be no difficulty in finding the rising place.

Weaknesses and wounds: Lost her head – but this was buried with her, so it'll be within reach.

Extra facts and zombie quotes: The chapel also contains the remains of a number of other doubtless aggrieved corpses, including Sir Thomas More, Thomas Cromwell, and Henry's fifth wife, Catherine Howard. Plus there are approximately twenty-nine other aristocrats and nobles buried here, each of whom was convicted of treason or similar crimes between 1530 and 1747. Overall, this part of the Tower of London will be hoaching with zombies bearing some serious grudges.

Difficulty rating:

HENRY VIII,
KING OF ENGLAND
1491–1547

Height: At least 6ft, with a well-proportioned muscular body to match (until he turned into a mammoth in his later years).

Age at death: 55.

Special skills: Disposing of wives (beheaded two out of six); making war (France, Scotland, Ireland); jousting and sports (he was a skilled athlete); music and poetry (he was well-read and creative); initiating the English Reformation (partly because the Pope wouldn't grant him a divorce); building the modern English nation; and executing anyone who annoyed him.

What killed him? Obesity, combined with kidney and liver failure. Probably. Henry's multiple symptoms in his later life have attracted extensive medical analysis, none of which can be absolutely verified. Some of his conditions – the lapses in memory, the extreme mood swings, and the transition from a handsome, virile hunk into a monstrously fat ogre – suggest an endocrine abnormality. Diabetes is another possibility. He also spent large sums on perfumes to disguise the offensive smells from his ulcerated legs.

Where is he buried? St George's Chapel, Windsor Castle, next to the body of his third queen, Jane Seymour, who died shortly after giving birth to the future Edward VI.

Weaknesses and wounds: The younger Henry was as fit as they come; older Henry was an entire medical textbook, and so grotesquely enlarged that he needed mechanical devices to move him around.

Extra facts and zombie quotes: For the funeral procession from London, Henry's elephantine body was, with some difficulty, placed in its coffin, and transported with a life-size effigy on top. During an overnight stop at Syon, parts of the lead coffin burst open, so that 'all the pavement of the church was with the fat and the corrupt and putrefied blood foully imbued'. A dog lapped up some of the royal goo, and the metal was soldered shut again. When the vault at Windsor was opened in 1888, Henry's coffin was found badly damaged. This may have been caused when the overweight coffin fell off its trestle, but commentators thought at the time that the king's vast body had exploded once more.

Difficulty rating: 💀

MARY I,
QUEEN OF ENGLAND
1516–1558

Height: 'She is of low rather than of middling stature, but, although short, she has not personal defect in her limbs, nor is any part of her body deformed.' So wrote the Venetian ambassador in 1557.

Age at death: 42.

Special skills: Burning Protestants and generally alienating the English nation. When her Protestant brother Edward IV died, Catholic Mary was a hugely popular choice for the throne and easily triumphed over the nine-day reign of the hapless Lady Jane Grey. By the end of her life Mary, having married a widely disliked and opportunistic Spanish prince, lost the last English possession in France (Calais) and burned hundreds of Protestant martyrs, was mourned by just a few. Later generations bestowed the name 'Bloody Mary', and the appellation has stuck.

What killed her? Probably uterine or cervical cancer.

Where is she buried? Westminster Abbey, although her heart and bowels were buried in the Chapel Royal of St James's Palace. The much-damaged and repaired plaster head from her funeral effigy is kept in the abbey's Undercroft Museum.

Weaknesses and wounds: Because of the bitter soap opera that was the life and loves of Henry VIII and his search for the right wife (and heir), Mary, unusually for the time, was not married off for dynastic advantage. Indeed, she did not take a husband until the age of 38 – at which point she desperately needed to have a child, if only to ensure that England would remain on the new Catholic course she had embarked upon. Her belly bloomed and a

royal birth-to-be was joyfully proclaimed – but then she slimmed down, and there was no baby. A second false pregnancy simply highlighted the menstrual and abdominal problems she suffered for much of her life.

Extra facts and zombie quotes: Better known as 'Bloody Mary', the re-animated Mary will be no stranger to the sight of disembowelled corpses and burning flesh. She also has a terrifying name to boot.

Difficulty rating:

MARY,
QUEEN OF SCOTS
1542–1587

Height: Possibly 5ft 11ins, very tall for a woman of the period.

Age at death: 44.

Special skills: Mary's accomplishments have largely been overshadowed by the hypnotising drama of her life – and propaganda, lies, religious prejudice and fantasy surround the stories told of her. At one point she held the fate of both Scotland and England in her hands, but she spent the last nineteen years of her life as a *de facto* prisoner in various English castles. Eventually she was condemned for being part of a conspiracy to assassinate Elizabeth I – which she may or may not have been involved in. Good at sending coded messages, and possibly assassinating husbands.

What killed her? The executioner, Bull, guided her to the low block on the scaffold at Fotheringay Castle in Northamptonshire and swung his short-handled woodman's axe. Everyone present was nervous, terrified that something in the stage-management of this crucial execution would go wrong, and the tension rubbed off on Bull. His first stroke only hit the back of Mary's head. The next blow severed the neck almost entirely, except for a piece of sinew which Bull cut through. A grotesquely comic moment occurred when Bull held up the head – and was left clutching only an auburn wig as Mary's grey-haired cranium fell to the floor.

Where is she buried? Mary lay inside a lead coffin within the hall at Fotheringay, locked up for five months while Elizabeth's government worked out what to do with the inconvenient corpse. Eventually Mary was laid to rest at Peterborough Cathedral.

Twenty-five years later, in 1612, Catholic Mary was moved to Protestant Westminster Abbey, interred among people who had often been her enemies.

Weaknesses and wounds: Apart from the small issue of a severed head, Mary was weakened by several recurrent illnesses.

Extra facts and zombie quotes: In 1869 a royal coffin-hunt (they had misplaced James I) entered the vault beneath the tomb. 'A startling, it may be said awful, scene presented itself,' wrote the Dean of Westminster. Mary's huge coffin was badly compressed by the weight of the coffins lying on top of it, but the lead had not actually burst. Even so, it's going to be tough getting out from beneath all that weight.

Difficulty rating:

SIR FRANCIS DRAKE,
SEA CAPTAIN
c. 1540–1596

Height: Perhaps about 5ft 2ins.

Age at death: 55, probably.

Special skills: The greatest seaman of the Tudor Age. His voyage around the world on the *Golden Hind* filled the Treasury with looted Spanish gold, and his daring Pearl Harbor-type attack on the Spanish fleet in Cadiz harbour, wherein he 'singed the King of Spain's beard', made him a national hero (the Africans who he sold as slaves in the West Indies may have had other opinions, of course). Drake was part of Elizabeth I's 'Black Ops', committing acts of terrorism while operating at arm's length from the government. A pirate in all but name, Drake's haul of gold and silver disabled the Spanish economy – and made him incredibly rich. Later, he was the hero of the defeat of the Spanish Armada and became the most famous man in Elizabethan England, leaving a legacy of mysteries, from secret landfalls in California to buried treasure and lost ships.

What killed him? Dysentery or a similar disease, acquired on yet another treasure-seeking voyage in the Spanish Main.

Where is he buried? This is one zombie you're not going to locate easily. Drake was buried at sea, deposited in full armour off the coast of Portobello, Panama, in an undisclosed location. You *could* hire a boat and wait around above one of the several places Drake-nuts have identified as the true, real, genuine, authentic, honest-to-goodness, sea-bed burial site. Or you could just pop along to the full-size replica of the *Golden Hind* near London Bridge, pick up a cutlass, and see what transpires.

Weaknesses and wounds: Drake was wounded several times during his battles, on one occasion so severely that his crew abandoned the treasure to ensure his survival. However, the fact that, after decades at sea and at war, he was still raiding and fighting at the age of 55, speaks volumes about his constitution.

Extra facts and zombie quotes: Drake was the kind of man who could behead a mutinous seaman (see above), keep his cool in the midst of a mass sea battle, and, Shackleton-like, save his men from near-death by performing heroic acts of navigation and endurance. Do you really want a piece of him?

Difficulty rating:

ELIZABETH I,
QUEEN OF ENGLAND
1533–1603

Height: Perhaps between 5ft 3ins and 5ft 5ins.

Age at death: 69.

Special skills: The daughter of Henry VIII (see p. 74) and Anne Boleyn (see p. 72), and queen for an incredible forty-four years, Elizabeth saw off endless plots and conspirators, defeated the military juggernaut of Spain and its Armada, juggled religious and political factions, and generally wrote herself into the history books as England's greatest queen and one of the most famous Britons ever. She's also quite likely to be able to kill you with her bare hands.

What killed her? Probably pneumonia exacerbated by a severe infection of the mouth and gums.

Where is she buried? She died in Richmond on 24 March. The body was embalmed and interred in Westminster Abbey a month later; Elizabeth's heart was removed and enclosed in a casket alongside that of her sister, Queen Mary I.

Weaknesses and wounds: Elizabeth had been hit by smallpox earlier in life and in her later years was prey to many of the infirmities of old age.

Extra facts and zombie quotes: As she said at Tilbury camp, at the very moment when invasion was expected, 'I know I have but the body of a weak and feeble woman, but I have the heart and stomach of a King.' There's only one way to find out!

Difficulty rating: 🖤

Historical disclaimer: In her old age 'Gloriana' was a mobile masquerade of wigs and cosmetics, all designed to disguise her ravaged features. Will she refuse to rise from her tomb unless she gets some decent make-up?

GUY FAWKES,
GUNPOWDER PLOT CONSPIRATOR

1570–1606

Height: His exact height is unknown, but he is described as tall and powerfully built.

Age at death: 35.

Special skills: Yorkshire-born Guy 'Guido' Fawkes was a man of action: a militant Catholic, he had fought skilfully for the Spanish against the Protestant Dutch. When a cabal of English Catholics plotted to assassinate the Protestant King James I, Fawkes was brought in as the explosives expert, a direct consequence of his military experience. The Gunpowder Plot, had it succeeded, would have been the seventeenth century's 9/11, killing not just the king and the nobles, but the many ordinary Londoners who gathered to see the Opening of Parliament: mass murder on a grand scale.

What killed him? Guido was one tough *hombre*. He resisted interrogation, only breaking down after prolonged torture via the manacles and the rack. On the day of his execution, at Old Palace Yard, Westminster, he was drawn through the streets behind a horse head downwards, but managed to cheat the final punishment – having his testicles cut off and his guts opened while still alive – by throwing himself off the scaffold, thereby breaking his neck.

Where is he buried? This is where you, gentle zombie-hunter, may have a problem. Fawkes' limbs were cut off and displayed as a warning to others in 'the four corners of the kingdom' – but we are not told where. His trunk was probably thrown into the Thames, but it may have been disposed of in a pit – we are not told. As for his head – we don't know about that either.

Weaknesses and wounds: Tortured and cut into pieces – he's not going to be in good shape. May also have a problem if you want an autograph.

Extra facts and zombie quotes: When asked why he wanted to kill the king, Fawkes replied: 'A desperate disease requires a dangerous remedy'. Zombie-hunters, take note.

Difficulty rating:

Historical disclaimer: If you do manage to locate the fellow's parts, then you will earn the undying gratitude of historians – who, however, might be a tad busy dealing with their own quarter of the zombie apocalypse.

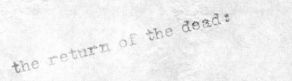

the return of the dead:

SIR ROBERT LOGAN (1609)

In 1609 Sir Robert Logan was on trial for treason in Edinburgh. He made a poor job of his defence, possibly because he had been dead for three years. His corpse was propped up in court, and found guilty of attempting to murder James I (James VI of Scotland) during the Gowrie Conspiracy of 1600. The Logans of Restalrig were par for the course when it came to Scottish nobles – greedy, unpleasant thugs. The verdict of treason meant they were stripped of their titles and property, with the Crown conveniently becoming correspondingly wealthier.

the return of the dead:

THOMAS GREY (1608)

'In the reign of King James, at Astley in Warwickshire, upon the fall of the church, there was taken up the corpse of Thomas Grey, Marquis of Dorset, who was there buried the tenth of October, 1530, in the twenty-second year of King Henry the Eighth; and although it had lain seventy-eight years in this bed of corruption, yet his eyes, hair, flesh, nails, and joints, remained as if he had been but newly buried.'

Joseph Taylor, *The danger of premature interment* (1816)

Thomas Grey was Lady Jane Grey's grandfather. If he isn't at the church, likely places to get him include the house here, Bradgate, his beloved mansion in Leicestershire. Since he was a warrior, a jousting champion, a veteran of battlefields across England and France and an ex-jailbird to boot, you might want to take some armour. And a gun.

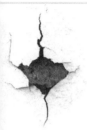

WILLIAM SHAKESPEARE,

PLAYWRIGHT

1564–1616

Height: Unknown – like most things about Shakespeare, who, as with most people of his time, has only the barest minimum of biographical material on record.

Age at death: 52.

Special skills: When it came to the business of writing plays, not too shabby. But if you think you're dealing with a wimp, think again. A court document from 1596 shows that one William Wayte 'swore before the Judge of Queen's Bench that he stood in danger of death, or bodily hurt' from William Shakespeare and three others. Other records from the same period show that this was part of a turf war between two gangsters, each running a disreputable theatre (where the profits often came from prostitution and crime). Was 'Stratford Bill' a bit tasty? It's intriguing to think so.

What killed him? Unknown.

Where is he buried? Holy Trinity church, Stratford-upon-Avon. The grave monument has a curse inscribed on it, which in modern English reads:

> Good friend, for Jesus' sake forbear,
> To dig the dust enclosed here.
> Blessed be the man that spares these stones,
> And cursed be he that moves my bones.

Weaknesses and wounds: Unknown.

Extra facts and zombie quotes: The Bard is purpose-built for the aspiring actor wishing to add a suitable quote to the combat. Try:

'Tis a consummation devoutly to be wished.' (*Hamlet*)

'Death, a necessary end, will come when it will come.' (*Julius Caesar*)

'Be absolute for death; either death or life shall thereby be the sweeter.' (*Measure for Measure*)

'Woe, destruction, ruin, and decay; the worst is death, and death will have his day.' (*Richard II*)

'Doomsday is near; die all, die merrily.' (*Henry IV, Part I*)

'Death, death; oh, amiable, lovely death! Come, grin on me, and I will think thou smilest.' (*King John*)

Then we have the scene from *Hamlet* where the prince sees his deceased father:

> Tell why thy canonized bones, hearsed in death,
> Have burst their cerements; why the sepulchre,
> Wherein we saw thee quietly inurn'd,
> Hath opened his ponderous and marble jaws, To cast thee up again!
> What may this mean,
> That thou, dead corpse, again, in complete steel,
> Revisit'st thus the glimpses of the moon?

Difficulty rating: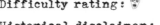

Historical disclaimer: You'll have only yourself to blame if Bill gets a bit narky when you ask him whether it's true that Christopher Marlowe and/or Francis Bacon actually wrote his plays.

POCAHONTAS,
NATIVE VIRGINIAN
c. 1595-1617

Height: Unknown, but her people impressed the colonists as being taller than the English average.

Age at death: 21 or 22.

Special skills: Pocahontas was one of dozens of children born to the many wives of Wahunsonacock, the leader of a federation of coastal Native American tribes known as the Powhatan Confederacy. What distinguished her was her childhood willingness to spend time with the aliens who had arrived in their midst – the English colonists of Jamestown. In an event which probably didn't happen, she allegedly prevented her father from executing colonist John Smith. A few years later war broke out between Jamestown and the Powhatan. Pocahontas was kidnapped, learned English and married tobacco-grower John Rolfe, taking the name Rebecca. Her marriage helped broker a temporary peace between the two peoples.

What killed her? Pocahontas was the perfect advert for the faltering colony – the 'good Indian' whose conversion to Christianity was an emblem that the New World could be tamed and rendered fit for English civilisation. She, her husband and their son John were consequently brought to England, where she was well-treated, even if regarded as little more than a curiosity, and, in a fine piece of advertising *legerdemain*, her status as a chief's daughter was elevated to that of 'princess'. Potential investors in the Virginia colony were satisfied that the natives, as exemplified by the English-speaking 'Lady Rebecca', would be biddable and pliant. Returning to America with her husband, Pocahontas was taken ill while still in the Thames Estuary. She died from an unknown disease.

Where is she buried? St George's church, Gravesend, Kent. A statue stands in the grounds, but the exact location of the grave is unknown.

Weaknesses and wounds: Other than her final illness, we know nothing of her medical history.

Extra facts and zombie quotes: You have to hope that the undead Pocahontas has not learned what subsequently happened to the Native Americans, and has not seen the history-corrupting animated film named after her. If she has, then she is going to be a very disaffected zombie indeed.

Difficulty rating:

SIR WALTER RALEIGH, EXPLORER

c. 1552–1618

Height: 6ft.

Age at death: About 66.

Special skills: Raleigh's famous exploits in exploring the coasts of North and South America have eclipsed certain of his military actions, such as fighting for the Huguenots in France, ruthlessly stamping out rebellions in Ireland – including massacring a garrison – and waging a fierce three-hour sea battle in the harbour of Cadiz. Despite his debonair exterior and his learning – he wrote poetry and history – Raleigh was steely ambition personified.

What killed him? Raleigh had the misfortune to outlive both the Tudor Age and Elizabeth herself. Her successor, the Stuart King James I, was not a fan. Raleigh became a politically expedient sacrifice to James' *rapprochement* with Spain. Following a show trial for treason, Raleigh was beheaded in the Old Palace Yard at the Palace of Westminster.

Where is he buried? Raleigh's last letter to his wife states: 'Beg my dead body which living was denied thee; and either lay it at Sherburne [his home in Dorset] ... or in Exeter.' This did not happen. The body was interred in St Margaret's church, Westminster, while his severed head was embalmed and given to his wife, who kept it in a velvet bag until her death twenty-nine years later. The head is buried beneath the organ of St Mary's church at West Horsley in Surrey, close to the Raleigh family home. A few years ago St Margaret's quietly asked St Mary's if they could have the head, to complete the set, so to speak; the request was politely declined.

Weaknesses and wounds: Apart from a leg wound acquired in the attack on Cadiz, there is the small matter that skull and torso are currently 26 miles apart. Will the body of the great explorer voyage along the A24 to locate its head?

Extra facts and zombie quotes: Raleigh asked the executioner to show him the axe. When the man hesitated, Raleigh said, 'Dost thou think I am afraid of it?' Testing the edge with his thumb, the old adventurer quipped, 'This is sharp medicine, but it will cure all diseases.' This was more than apt, as Raleigh had started to shake from a recurrent fever, and, as he said, 'I would not have my enemies think I quaked from fear.' His last words were, 'Strike, man, strike!'

Difficulty rating:

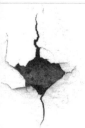

JAMES I,
KING OF ENGLAND, IRELAND AND SCOTLAND

1566–1625

Height: 'Of middling height', so probably around 5ft 5ins.

Age at death: 58.

Special skills: Survival. His mother was Mary, Queen of Scots (executed), his father Lord Darnley (murdered). He became James VI of Scotland at the age of thirteen months, and grew up witnessing the internecine violence of a country plagued by factions and civil war. In 1603, on the death of Elizabeth, he succeeded to the throne of England, 'Scotch Jimmy' thereby becoming both James VI of Scotland and James I of England. He weathered one kidnap (the Raid of Ruthven, 1582) and two assassination attempts (the Gowrie Conspiracy, 1600, and the Gunpowder Plot, 1605). The fact that he lived to old age was almost a miracle. Along the way, he persecuted witches, commissioned the King James Bible, largely avoided war, and spent huge sums on the young men to whom he was attracted.

What killed him? A series of illnesses which marred his final years, possibly including tuberculosis, kidney stones, arthritis, gout and other conditions.

Where is he buried? Westminster Abbey. The coffin was lost for 250 years, until it was located in the vault of Henry VII's tomb, complete with the initials of the gravediggers who, for some unknown reason, placed James's coffin in its unrecorded final resting place.

Weaknesses and wounds: Before his later illnesses he was physically fit, spending many of the daylight hours hunting stags.

Extra facts and zombie quotes: After he died, his 'body and head swelled beyond measure, the hair with the skin of the

head stuck to the pillow, and the nails became loose upon the fingers and toes.' All this suggests that he had arsenic in his system. Some claimed the Duke of Buckingham, who had given him an unspecified white powder, had poisoned James. The *Harleian Miscellany*, written many years later, claimed that Buckingham told the king's doctors to sign a writ that the powder was 'a good safe medicine', but they refused. Certainly James got worse after taking the powder, but this does not mean it was poison – he could simply have been on the way out anyway, and many people had good reason to blacken the name of Buckingham, one of James' former favourites. This was a royal court, after all.

Difficulty rating:

the return of the dead:

CONSTANCE WHITNEY (1628) AND A HOST OF OTHER 'LADIES WITH THE RING'

Before it was destroyed in the Blitz, you could find a memorial to a revenant in a London church. Well, apparently. The monument was in St Giles church, Cripplegate, and was erected in memory of Constance Whitney, who died in 1628 at the age of 17. Its carving of the young Constance emerging from her winding sheet prompted an expansive folklore which claimed that the sculpture did not represent the Resurrection on Judgement Day, but was a literal rendering of Constance Whitney's real-life rise from the tomb. According to the galloping legend – which picked up pace and new details every time it was retold – Constance was buried with an expensive ring. A greedy sexton opened her coffin and tried to prise the jewel from her finger. It stuck, so he became a bit rough – at which point Constance, who was not really dead but in a coma, woke up, her apparent return from the dead scaring the scavenger off. By the time vampire enthusiast and all-round eccentric Montague Summers got hold of it in 1928, the tale had mutated into that of a veritable vampire or zombie, and several modern writers who should know better have also been seduced by the story. It is, however, a load of old hooey.

The tale of Constance Whitney's accidental resurrection at the hands of a thief is in fact just one of hundreds of variants on an enduring folk-tale known as 'the Lady with the Ring', also known in the International Index of Folklore Motifs as Tale Type 990, 'the Lady Restored to Life'.

HAROLD II,
KING OF ENGLAND
1022–1066

Height: He is described as 'very tall … remarkable for his physical strength.'

Age at death: 44.

Special skills: Harold has had a bit of a bad press, being largely remembered as the loser at the Battle of Hastings. In fact, long before he was king, Harold Godwinsone had the blood-drenched swagger of an Anglo-Saxon Al Capone, annexing territories, disposing of rivals, and slaughtering on a vast scale. His scorched-earth response to a rebellion in North Wales left, as one chronicler out it, 'not one that pisseth against a wall.' In 1066 he led his army on an incredible forced march to Yorkshire, where they annihilated a Viking force led by his estranged brother Tostig and the Norwegian king Harold Hardrada, easily one of the fiercest warriors who ever lived. A few weeks later, after another astonishing forced march, Harold faced-off against William the Bastard's Norman invasion. The contest lasted nine hours, one of the longest battles in the Middle Ages. Harold had been king for nine months; his death marked the eclipse of Anglo-Saxon England.

What killed him? Probably a fatal arrow in the face, but it is said he was also hacked apart by four of William's knights. Very likely both things happened.

Where is he buried? The traditional site is Waltham Abbey in Essex, where a marker cautiously reads: 'This stone marks the position of the high altar behind which King Harold is said to have been buried 1066.' However, a body discovered at Bosham church near Chichester in 1954 exactly matches the wounds Harold is said to have suffered (see below).

Weaknesses and wounds: Extensive – if he reanimates, this is going to be one splenetic Saxon. Firstly, there's that famous arrow. Then there's the fact that his head and right leg were chopped off and taken away, and the left leg cut off at the knee. Add to that the fact that his body was so mutilated it could only be identified amidst the piles of corpses by his mistress, Edith Swan-neck, who recognised marks on the skin 'known only to her'.

Extra facts and zombie quotes: Least likely to say: 'It's all fun and games until somebody loses an eye'. Most likely to say: 'You bastard!'

Difficulty rating:

RICHARD III,
KING OF ENGLAND
1452–1485

Height: 5ft 8ins, but severe scoliosis of the spine would have made him much shorter, perhaps by as much as twelve inches.

Age at death: 33.

Special skills: Courage – he was fighting battles in desperate close combat by the age of eighteen; martial ability – skilled with axe, sword and lance; leadership – he led many successful military campaigns; and ruthlessness – he never shirked from executing anyone deemed inconvenient, from opposing nobles and Lancastrian rebels to members of his own family (notably the Princes in the Tower). Richard generally made a poor showing as king, but as a warrior he was death incarnate.

What killed him? At Bosworth Field, Richard became the last king of England to die in battle. He launched a cavalry charge against the retinue of his rival, Henry Tudor, personally unhorsing jousting champion Sir John Cheney, cutting down Henry's bear-like standard-bearer William Brandon and coming within killing distance of Henry himself, before being overwhelmed. The razor-sharp blade of a halberd slashed off the rear of his skull, while a sword cut through his face into his brain.

Where is he buried? In an incredible archaeological find, his bones, long since thought lost, were located in 2012 in a car park in Leicester. If you want to take on Richard now, you'll have to head to his new home, Leicester Cathedral, where it is hoped he will be in residence from 2014.

Weaknesses and wounds: The body was stripped naked and displayed on the back of a horse: there are numerous small post-mortem wounds, the type that typically come from the abuse of a

body. Someone even pushed a dagger into his arse. In addition, the skeleton is lacking the feet, these having been lost when another grave was cut through the long-forgotten royal remains. So he's going to be slow, short – and angry.

Extra facts and zombie quotes: A ballad of the time described Richard saying on the day of his death:

> Give me my battle-axe in hand
> And set my crown on my head so high,
> For by him that made both sun and moon,
> King of England this day I will die!

With his glorious but futile cavalry charge died the Plantagenet dynasty, and indeed the Middle Ages. No future king would dare ride into battle so recklessly.

Difficulty rating:

NAPOLEON III,
EMPEROR OF THE FRENCH
1808–1873

Height: About 5ft 6ins, with short legs. An order for his arrest included: 'Special peculiarities: head sunk into shoulders, arched back.'

Age at death: 64.

Special skills: Ruling the French (never an easy task). There aren't many opportunities to take on a Gallic celebrity zombie on these shores, and Napoleon III is your best bet. While nineteenth-century Britain prospered under the long and stable reign of Victoria, France went through a bewildering number of short-lived regimes. Having lived most of his life in exile, fought for Italian nationalists in his youth, and attempted two pathetic coups, Louis-Napoleon, the nephew of Napoleon Bonaparte, finally became the elected President of France in 1848. Three years later he ousted the Republicans and autocratically declared himself Napoleon III, Emperor of France. The Second Empire re-established France's status as a European power, with military adventures in the Crimea and Italy, and the creation of a modern industrial economy. Despite having been a very competent artillery officer in the Swiss army, the emperor had no skill as a general; his personal leadership of the army in the Franco-Prussian War of 1870 was an utter disaster.

What killed him? He died under the surgeon's knife, during an operation to remove a bladder stone.

Where is he buried? The would-be ruler had lived in both Leamington Spa (Warwickshire) and Southport (Lancashire) during his wilderness years. After 1871 his exile was Chislehurst in Kent.

Having been originally buried in the Catholic church there, in 1888 his remains were moved to the new St Michael's Abbey in Farnborough (Hampshire). His casket can be seen in the Imperial Crypt.

Weaknesses and wounds: Napoleon III was not a well man; in middle-age he suffered from diseases of the kidneys, bladder and prostate, as well as arthritis and gout. He dragged his left leg.

Extra facts and zombie quotes: The emperor's funeral and Lying in State quite overwhelmed the small village of Chislehurst, leading to an extensive account in *The Graphic* newspaper:

> Little, however, can be learnt by gazing on the face of the dead, because the man, whose vitality once gave expression to those features, is no longer there, and this senseless Thing, to which we do honour, is a mere waxen effigy of the original.

Difficulty rating: 💀

the return of the dead:

JOHN WYCLIFFE (1428)

Forty-four years after he died, John Wycliffe was dug up from his grave in Lutterworth, Leicestershire.

Chances of adding him to the target list are slim, however, as whatever remained of him was burned, and his ashes thrown into the River Swift. His crime was to criticise and attempt to reform the Catholic Church. For this he was found guilty of heresy, although the verdict was only handed down more than thirty years after his death. His books were burned immediately, but it took another thirteen years for the vengeful Church to get round to his body.

ALICE HACKNEY (1495)

'At the digging of a new foundation in the church of Saint Mary Hill in London, there was then found and taken up the body of Alice Hackney: she had been buried in that church 175 years before; yet was she then found whole of skin, and the joints of her arms pliable; her corpse was kept above ground four days without any inconvenience, exposed to the view of as many as would behold it, and then recommitted to the earth.'

Richard Baker, *Chronicle of the Kings of England* (1643)

Although the names and the places change, the core story is always the same. In his excellent book *Buried Alive*, Jan Bondeson traces the first sighting of the tale to the first or second century AD in ancient Greece, and during the seventeenth century there were dozens of versions in Germany, France, Italy, Scandinavia, Switzerland – and of course Britain. In 2008 I stood listening to an Aberdeenshire tour guide tell *exactly the same story* in relation to Meriorie Elphinston of Inverurie, who died in 1622. Other 'Ladies with the Ring' in the British Isles include:

- Annot of Benallay (Cornwall) – the earliest British Lady with the Ring, dating from the fourteenth century.

- Ladies from two generations of the Wyndham family in Somerset.

- Ladies from two generations of the Edgcumbe family in Cornwall.

- Eliza Fanshawe of Woodley Hall (Gloucestershire).

- Margaret Halcrow Erskine (Berwickshire).

- Hannah Goodman (County Cork).

- Mrs Harrison of Drogheda (County Lough).

- Marjorie MacCall (County Armagh) – her gravestone says 'Lived Once, Buried Twice.'

- The miller's wife of Rudby (Yorkshire).

- One of the Lindsays of Edzell (Angus).

None of them were woken from a death-like coma by a ring-stealing ruffian. None were vampires, zombies or revenants. Get a grip, people.

the return of the dead:

JOHN BARTENDALE (1634)

Piper and wandering minstrel Bartendale was hanged on open country-side outside Mickelgate Bar in York. After dangling for about forty-five minutes he was cut down, declared dead, and hastily buried at the foot of the gallows.

Some time later – we are not told how long – a Mr Vavasour and his servant, who happened to be passing, saw a strange movement in the earth. They uncovered Bartendale, who sat up and asked how he had got there, as well he might. The man was naked, his clothes having been stripped and sold, so Mr Vavasour wrapped him in his cloak. At the next assizes in York the judge, being disinclined to reverse the verdict of Providence, set Bartendale free, and the man thereafter appears to have led a blameless life.

the return of the dead:

THE WOMEN OF OXFORD (1650 & 1658)

Both Anne Green (1650) and 'Elizabeth the servant' (1658) were hanged at Oxford, and both revived soon after, despite each hanging for a long time and enduring additional violence (Anne was stamped on and hit with a musket in an effort to finish her off, while Elizabeth fell from the high gallows). Anne was pardoned and lived another nineteen years, but Elizabeth was executed (again) the following day.

OLIVER CROMWELL,
LORD PROTECTOR
1599-1658

Height: About 6ft.

Age at death: 59.

Special skills: You are a minor member of the country gentry with absolutely no military experience. At the advanced age of 43 you form a small body of mounted troops to fight in the Civil War. Soon you are winning battles, leading the entire New Model Army and eventually executing a king and turning England into a republic. You are Oliver Cromwell, and you are one of the most controversial men in history.

What killed him? Probably septicaemia (blood poisoning) brought about by a severe kidney infection.

Where is he buried? The body was poorly embalmed, and became rank with putrefaction: 'It purged and wrought through all, so that there was a necessity of interring it before the Solemnity of his Funeral,' wrote his physician. At some point the noisome cadaver was quietly buried in Westminster Abbey, long before the grand funeral, which was centred on an effigy of wood and wax and an empty coffin. That should have been that, but more than two years later, after the Restoration of Charles II, Cromwell's body was dug up, and taken to the execution site at Tyburn to be posthumously hanged and mutilated. The remains were then thrown into an unmarked pit, which means your target is somewhere beneath the Marble Arch junction, possibly around Connaught Street or Connaught Square. But that's not all; Cromwell's head was severed and displayed on a pole at Westminster Hall. When it blew down in a storm (or was stolen) the head passed through various hands as a grim collector's piece before, in 1960, being interred in a secret location within the ante-chapel of Sidney Sussex College, Cambridge. So, once again, we have a 'body in one place, head in another' scenario. What's a put-upon zombie hunter to do?

Weaknesses and wounds: Cromwell's health declined after a bout of malaria. Other than that he was in fine fettle, so if he manages to round up any re-animated remnants of Oliver's Army, then watch out...

Extra facts and zombie quotes: On his deathbed, Cromwell was asked whether he wished to drink and then rest. His reply became his final words: 'It is not my design to drink or to sleep, but my design is to make what haste I can to be gone.'

Difficulty rating:

Historical disclaimer: There are at least half-a-dozen other places in England that claim to hold the 'true' grave of Oliver Cromwell...

the return of the dead:

THE REGICIDES OF CHARLES I (1660)

It wasn't just Cromwell who was dug up and 'punished' after his death. John Bradshaw and Henry Ireton, two of the other Commissioners who had signed the death warrant of Charles I, were also disinterred, taken to the execution ground at Tyburn, hanged and beheaded. Like Cromwell, their bodies were then deposited in a pit, and their heads spiked outside Westminster Hall – the very building where the Commissioners had condemned the king to death. Unlike Cromwell, however, no tales were handed down about the fates of Bradshaw's and Ireton's heads. A similar post-mortem fate was intended for the body of Thomas Pride, but his corpse had decayed too much to be 'punished'.

The vengeance against the regicides was not confined to the already dead. One Commissioner was hanged, while twelve were hung, drawn and quartered, and nineteen were sentenced to life imprisonment.

the return of the dead:

THE PLAGUE PIPER (1665)

The cart came to the place where the bodies were to be thrown into the ground … as soon as the cart stopped the fellow awaked and struggled a little to get his head out from among the dead bodies, when, raising himself up in the cart, he called out, 'Hey! where am I?' This frighted the fellow that attended about the work; but after some pause John Hayward, recovering himself, said, 'Lord, bless us! There's somebody in the cart not quite dead!' So another called to him and said, 'Who are you?' The fellow answered, 'I am the poor piper. Where am I?' 'Where are you?' says Hayward. 'Why, you are in the dead-cart, and we are going to bury you.' 'But I ain't dead though, am I?' says the piper, which made them laugh a little though, as John said, they were heartily frighted at first; so they helped the poor fellow down, and he went about his business.

Daniel Defoe, *Journal of a Plague Year*

The Great Plague of 1665 saw several similar episodes. In one, a butcher from Newgate Market, left for dead but not picked up by the plague cart, revived during the night, complaining only that he felt cold.

the return of the dead:

ROBERT BRAYBOOK (1666)

The Great Fire of London destroyed St Paul's Cathedral, in the process disinterring Robert Braybrook, Bishop of London, who, despite having been in the grave for 262 years, was found still in possession of his skin, hair, joints and nails. 'His body was exposed to the view of all sorts of people for divers days; and some thousands did behold and pose it in their arms, till by special order it was reinterred.' (Nathaniel Wanley, *The Wonders of the Little World: Or, A General History of Man, Displaying the Various Faculties, Capacities, Powers and Defects of the Human Body and Mind*, 1806)

the return of the dead:

MADAM BLUNDEN (1674)

This 'fat gross woman' from Basingstoke fell into a stupor after consuming opium water and was declared dead. Her body stank so badly that she was very quickly buried. Two days after the funeral, noises and cries were heard coming from the grave. It took two days for the authorities to decide to exhume the body, which turned out to be badly bruised from her attempts to escape the coffin. Declared dead once again, she was left in the closed coffin beside the grave – but apparently revived again during the night, the body being found the next day with more signs of a struggle. This time, however, she had definitely expired. An inquest was held, and the town of Basingstoke was levied with a large fine for its carelessness. Based on our improved understanding of the changes in the human body after death, it seems likely that the noises heard were caused by gas escaping from the huge and bloated body, while the 'bruisings' and other wounds are consistent with post-mortem changes in the newly deceased corpse, especially where decomposition has rapidly set in.

Citizens of Basingstoke, ask for your money back!

CHARLES II,
KING OF ENGLAND, IRELAND AND SCOTLAND

1630–1685

Height: 6ft 2ins.

Age at death: 54.

Special skills: Charm, cunning and concupiscence. Not much you may think, but consider the times. His father, Charles I, had lost his head to Cromwell's Puritan axe; his successor, his brother James II, was one of the most disastrous kings ever, losing both the throne and the Stuart monarchy. Charles II was hardly a warrior king, preferring the conquests of the bedroom, but, despite the Great Plague, the Great Fire of London, intermittent war with the Dutch, political duplicity, ghastly executions and religious rumblings, the Merry Monarch's reign was not too bad overall.

What killed him? Acute renal failure. During the five days of his final illness, Charles endured fifty-eight different drugs – including various vile enemas, a bezoar from a goat's stomach and 'spirits of human skull' – was bled, burned with irons and cupped with hot glasses, all of which probably contributed to his decline. Throughout these trials he maintained his good humour, telling his inept doctors: 'I am sorry, gentlemen, for being such a time a-dying.'

Where is he buried? The Henry VII Chapel in Westminster Abbey. The funeral was a modest affair, and for two centuries not even a name marked the grave. The vault was opened for maintenance in 1867 and again in 1977. On both occasions it was noted that the king's lead coffin had collapsed and the remains were visible.

Weaknesses and wounds: There is speculation that Charles may have had syphilis, which may have been responsible for the unpleasant ulcer on his leg. This cannot be proved, however. Perhaps you could ask him.

Extra facts and zombie quotes: A life-size wax figure stood beside the grave for many years. The fully dressed effigy is on display in the abbey's Undercroft Museum; the face, cast at death, shows the pain he was suffering.

Difficulty rating:

NELL GWYNN,
ROYAL MISTRESS
1650–1687

Height: Not known, but definitely 'short'.

Age at death: 37.

Special skills: Wit, acting, and sensuality. 'Pretty, witty Nell', as Samuel Pepys called her, was an illiterate child of the London streets who rose to become one of the greatest comic actresses of her age, and the devoted mistress of Charles II for sixteen years until his death in 1685. England loved her rags-to-riches story, and her personality – part reckless minx, part indiscreet gossip, part pert urchin, part comedienne – made her the Barbara Windsor of the Restoration.

What killed her? A stroke.

Where is she buried? St Martin-in-the-Fields, London. At the funeral the church was packed with ordinary Londoners remembering 'their Nell'.

Weaknesses and wounds: She may well have suffered from syphilis, although this is not certain.

Extra facts and zombie quotes: Generous, kind, fun-loving and funny, Nell is such an attractive historical figure you feel that deliberately taking her out would be uncharitable. Go off and hunt down some Norman nutjob instead, you unfeeling brute you.

Difficulty rating:

CAPTAIN KIDD,
PIRATE OF THE HIGH SEAS
1645 OR 1654–1701

Height: At his trial he was simply described as 'tall'.

Age at death: Somewhere between 47 and 56.

Special skills: Attacking ships. William Kidd first appears on record in 1689, as a skilled sailor fighting on behalf of the British Crown. After a tussle with the French, Captain Thomas Hewetson described Kidd as, 'A mighty man in the Caribbean … who fought as well as any man I ever saw'. In the murky legal world of the time, Kidd was regarded as a privateer, that is, a private individual whose attacks on enemy vessels were blessed by the British government. Any booty taken in the attacks was kept by Kidd: it was basically piracy by another name. In later life Kidd went on a privateering expedition to the Indian Ocean, ostensibly to hunt down pirates. Depending on who you believe, he either turned to piracy himself, or was duped and betrayed by his Establishment backers and eventually sacrificed. Or both.

What killed him? After his trial for piracy and murder, the alcoholic Kidd was filled with brandy and rum, paraded through the streets and hanged over the Thames mudflats at Execution Dock in Wapping. The first time the rope broke, and the befuddled and drunk man was pulled out of the mud to be hanged again. As the law demanded, his body hung on the gallows until three tides had washed over it.

Where is he buried? The body was tarred and hung inside a metal cage suspended above the shoreline, as an example to other sailors about the fate of pirates. When eventually cut down, the remains were probably consigned to the Thames off Tilbury Point.

Weaknesses and wounds: Broken neck, and two years of hanging in the gibbet and being pecked apart by birds.

Extra facts and zombie quotes: Kidd's acts of piracy were small beer compared to the depredations of other pirates; what made him famous was his 'treasure', a vast fortune cached in a secret location much hinted at during the trial, and which has obsessed treasure hunters ever since. Bet he won't tell you where he hid it, though.

Difficulty rating:

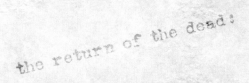

the return of the dead:

THE BODIES OF HOPE (1703)

On 14 January 1674 a farmer named Barber and his servant perished in a great snowstorm that covered the moors near Hope in Derbyshire. During that hard winter the snow lay on the ground for months, and the bodies were not discovered until 3 May, at which point they smelt so strongly that the coroner ordered them to be buried at the spot – which happened to be a peat moss.

Twenty-eight years and nine months later the bodies were dug up out of nothing more than curiosity – and found to be entirely preserved, looking as if they were newly dead. Mr Wermuld, the Minister of Hope, observed that: 'the flesh, when pressed with his finger, pitted a little, and the joints played freely, and without the least stiffness.' The bog bodies then became a local talking point, being kept around for about twenty years. In 1716 Dr Bourn of Chesterfield gave this account: 'the man perfect, his beard strong, and about a quarter of an inch long; the hair of his head short, his skin hard and of a tanned leather colour, pretty much the same as the liquor and earth they lay in. He had on a broad cloth coat, which he had tried to tear the skirt off, but could not.'

The woman was in a greater state of decay, having lost the flesh on one hand and leg and the tip of her nose. The bodies were eventually buried in Hope churchyard, and a subsequent investigation showed that they had entirely disintegrated there.

the return of the dead:

SIR WILLIAM LINDSAY (ABOUT 1687)

To all intents and purposes Sir William Lindsay of Covington in Angus died after a long illness. Just before the funeral, however, he revived. On being told that all and sundry had already arrived for the service, he decided to attend, especially as an ox had been slain for the feast. His return to life was kept secret, however, and it's fair to say the congregation were slightly surprised when the man they had come to mourn walked in through the door.

SIR ISAAC NEWTON,
PHYSICIST
1642–1727

Height: 5ft 6ins.

Age at death: 84.

Special skills: Being a genius. The laws of motion and of gravity, optics, mathematics, astronomy, mechanics ... Newton was the biggest brain on the physics front until Einstein came along 300 years later.

What killed him? It's not really clear; possibly bladder stones, although another possibility is mercury poisoning, a consequence of his practice of alchemy. Newton was at the same time the most brilliant rationalist of the period, and a devotee of religious mysticism, prophecies and magic.

Where is he buried? Westminster Abbey, where he was given a state funeral, an honour rarely granted to commoners. His death mask is held by the Royal Society.

Weaknesses and wounds: Newton was ill and frail in the period leading up to his death, although his mind was still sharp.

Extra facts and zombie quotes: Although by no means a conventional Christian, Newton studied the Bible intensively, writing extensive manuscripts that did not see the light of day until long after his death. In 1704 he assigned a series of assumed numbers to various Biblical elements and concluded that the apocalypse would not take place until at least 2060, although he probably meant not the actual destruction of the world, but the Second Coming of Christ. 'This I mention not to assert when the time of the end shall be,' he wrote, 'but to put a stop to the rash conjec-

tures of fanciful men who are frequently predicting the time of the end, and by doing so bring the sacred prophesies into discredit as often as their predictions fail.' One wonders what he will make of the zombacalyse. (N.B. As Newton made his most famous discovery after being hit by an apple, if you plan to give this zombie a try you should definitely consider braining him with a few well-aimed Braeburns before you charge. It would be wrong not to.)

Difficulty rating:

ROB ROY,
OUTLAW
1671–1734

Height: Unknown, but he had a reputation of being a big man with a long reach – helpful in a swordfight.

Age at death: 63.

Special skills: Swordsmanship, cattle rustling, blackmail and general roguery. He would have been a minor, long-forgotten bit-player in the endless clan feuds of the Scottish Highlands had one Daniel Defoe (author of *Robinson Crusoe*) not written a highly romanticised account of Rob's adventures while Rob was still alive. *Highland Rogue* provided the inspiration for Walter Scott's wildly popular *Rob Roy*, the two books between them creating a legend of a swashbuckling hero of the people, a Scottish Robin Hood. From the little we know of him, the real Rob Roy MacGregor was a typical man of his turbulent era: a respected cattle dealer when times were good, a bandit and blackmailer when times were bad. Various nobles seemed to have used him as a pawn or enforcer in their territorial enmities, and Roy had a reputation as a handy duellist and part-time hard man. His name alone was enough to inspire fear in less ferocious hearts. Tales of kidnaps, jailbreaks and spycraft added to the legend. Astonishingly, he lived to an old age and died at peace.

What killed him? Unknown, but probably illness.

Where is he buried? Balquidder, in Stirling District. His grave, much embellished on account of the legend, can still be seen in the churchyard.

Weaknesses and wounds: Unknown, although he may have been wounded in battle in 1719.

Extra facts and zombie quotes: Even in old age, Rob Roy was a force of nature. A story is told that a former foe came to see him while he was on his deathbed. Roy immediately got up and buckled on his sword. 'Never let it be said that any enemy of MacGregor ever saw him defenceless and unarmed', he said. Only when the unwelcome visitor had left did Rob collapse.

Difficulty rating:

the return of the dead:

WILLIAM DUELL (1740)

'William Duell was convicted of occasioning the death of Sarah Griffin, at Acton, by robbing and ill-treating her. Having suffered, 24th of November, 1740, at Tyburn … his body was brought to Surgeons' Hall to be anatomised; but after it was stripped and laid on the board, and one of the servants was washing it, in order to be cut, he perceived life in him, and found his breath to come quicker and quicker, on which a surgeon took some ounces of blood from him; in two hours he was able to sit up in his chair, and in the evening was again committed to Newgate, and his sentence, which might be again inflicted, was changed to transportation.' (*The Newgate Calendar*)

'It is evident from Experience, that many apparently dead, have afterwards proved themselves alive by rising from their shrouds, their coffins, and even from their graves.' (Jacques-Bénigne Winslow, *Morte incertae signa*, 1740)

DICK TURPIN,
HIGHWAYMAN

1705–1739

Height: 5ft 9in.

Age at death: 34.

Special skills: Ruthlessness in the pursuit of greed, with a tendency towards violence, torture and gunplay.

What killed him? He was hanged in York for horse theft, probably taking at least an hour to die of slow strangulation at the end of a short rope.

Where is he buried? Fishergate burial ground, York, with a clearly marked gravestone. The corpse was stolen by bodysnatchers, recovered, and then reburied.

Weaknesses and wounds: Bit of a sore neck.

Extra facts and zombie quotes: Far from the romantic legend of a handsome, charismatic and lovable rogue who made ladies' hearts flutter as he robbed them, Turpin was a loathsome scumbag. Pockmarked, ugly and coarse, with a strong sadistic streak, he graduated from sheep-, deer- and cattle-rustling in his native Essex to smuggling, housebreaking and, eventually, highway robbery. Often he informed on his colleagues to collect the reward, stole other smugglers' goods, and on one occasion he shot one of his compatriots and left him to the mercy of the authorities; the man was hanged. Householders and servants unfortunate enough to be targeted by his gang were subjected to great cruelty (including being forced onto the fire, mutilation and rape). After murdering a servant in Epping Forest, Turpin made his way north to Yorkshire under a pseudonym. The journey took several months, not the overnight ride of legend, and Turpin's horse Black Bess, who heartbreakingly died after faithfully galloping the 200 miles, never existed either – everything is a nineteenth-century invention. In Yorkshire he reverted to criminal type and ended on the gallows, finally behaving gallantly: 'With undaunted courage looked about him, and after speaking a few words to the topsman, he threw himself off the ladder.'

Difficulty rating:

Historical disclaimer: No dandy highwayman he, Turpin will likely not oblige you if you ask him to say, 'Stand and deliver!'

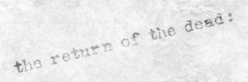

the return of the dead!

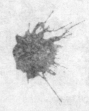

SIMON WORTH (1750)

A preserved body found in a vault in the church of St Paul de Leon at Staverton in Devon in 1750 created much excitement, with various people claiming it to be a miracle and removing parts of the covering material to use as healing relics. The individual concerned was Simon Worth, who had died in 1669, eighty-one years previously. Mr Tripe, surgeon, furnished the following description of the body to the *Philosophical Transactions*:

> When the vault was opened, about four months ago, it was found as perfect in all its parts as if but just interred. The whole body was plump and full, the skin white, soft, smooth and elastic; the hair strong, and the limbs nearly as flexible as when living.

The body had been wrapped in a winding-sheet and then enclosed in two coarse pitch-cloths. It was this pitch that had excluded the air and the usual agents of decay, while the curious fact that the oak coffin was below the water level in the Worth family vault seemed to have further contributed to the preservation. The vault filled with water every winter, and a large log and a heavy stone held down the coffin.

the return of the dead:

HANNAH BESWICK (1758)

The wealthy if slightly dotty Ms Beswick had a mortal fear of premature burial. In her will she left 20,000 guineas to her family physician, Dr Charles White, who was to ensure that (a) she was never to be buried and (b) her body was to be inspected regularly.

Dr White had his patient's remains embalmed and, every day over the course of several years, he and two reliable witnesses duly gazed on the corpse in case there were signs of life. After a while the body was kept in a grandfather clock, the face of which was opened just once a year, a procedure which continued until Dr White's death in 1813. The body made its way to the Manchester Natural History Museum where, as 'the Manchester Mummy' or 'the Mummy of Birchen Bower', it became much celebrated, with people peering through the glass case at the tightly bound body and black, shrivelled face. Ms Beswick's remains were finally buried in 1868, but not until the Secretary of State had issued an order dispensing with the legal requirement for a death certificate.

DR JOHNSON,
LITERARY TITAN
1709–1784

Height: 6ft.

Age at death: 75.

Special skills: Wit. Johnson is claimed to be the second most quoted person in the English language, after Shakespeare. His *A Dictionary of the English Language* made him one of the major celebrities of Georgian London. *A Life of Samuel Johnson,* the biography written by his friend James Boswell, cemented his status as one of the most mordantly incisive – and quotable – thinkers of his age. Having been often bitten by poverty himself, Johnson was frequently kind to those less well-off than himself. He was also – very unusually for his time – affectionately disposed towards animals. A statue of Hodge, his favourite cat, stands outside his house at 17 Gough Square in London. The idea of a zombie Johnson, surrounded by a legion of re-animated moggies, is an appealing one.

What killed him? Lung disease, heart disease and old age.

Where is he buried? Westminster Abbey.

Weaknesses and wounds: Johnson exhibited involuntary tics and convulsions, which have led to a recent diagnosis of Tourette's Syndrome. People encountering him for the first time often thought he was an idiot, a notion quickly disabused by his astounding eloquence.

Extra facts and zombie quotes: Johnson is irresistible on pretty much every subject. Consider the following, from Boswell's *Life*:

It matters not how a man dies, but how he lives. The act of dying is not of importance, it lasts so short a time.

Few believe it certain they are then to die; and those who do, set themselves to behave with resolution, as a man does who is going to be hanged. He is not the less unwilling to be hanged.

And to his doctor:

Sir, you cannot conceive with what acceleration I advance towards death.

Difficulty rating:

ROBERT BURNS,
POET
1759–1796

Height: 5ft 10ins, a good height for the period.

Age at death: 37.

Special skills: Poetry. When you sing 'Auld Lang Syne' at New Year, you're singing Burns. Masonry – he was initiated in the St David Tarbolton Lodge in 1781, so he'll have a definite old boys' club to draw on. X-ray or heat vision – possibly. (Walter Scott described his eye like so: 'It was large, and of a dark cast, and literally glowed when he spoke with feeling or interest. I never saw such another eye in a human head, though I have seen the most distinguished men of my time.')

What killed him? Victorian moralists embraced the idea that Burns had drunk himself to death. In fact, he seems to have been worn down by a combination of rheumatism, heart disease, fever and infection.

Where is he buried? His first resting place was a modest grave in St Michael's churchyard, in Dumfries. In 1817 his remains were reinterred in the much grander Burns Mausoleum nearby, the white-domed temple-like structure having been paid for by public subscription.

Weaknesses and wounds: His literary skills saved Burns from a lifetime of harsh manual labour, but his early farming experiences were so severe that they left a permanent effect on his health, including rheumatism and a weakness of the heart.

Extra facts and zombie quotes: The move of Burn's body to the mausoleum took place at midnight. William McDowall's *History of Dumfries* (1867) described what happened:

The lid removed, a spectacle was unfolded which, considering the fame of the mighty dead, has rarely been witnessed by a single human being. There were the remains of the great poet, to all appearance dearly entire, and retaining various traces of vitality, or rather exhibiting the features of one who had newly sunk into the sleep of death: the lordly forehead, arched and high, the scalp still covered with hair, and the teeth perfectly firm and white. The scene was so imposing that most of the workmen stood bare and uncovered ... and at the same time felt their frames thrilling with some undefinable emotion, as they gazed on the ashes of him whose fame is as wide as the world itself. But the effect was momentary; for when they proceeded to insert a shell or case below the coffin, the head separated from the trunk, and the whole body, with the exception of the bones, crumbled into dust.

In 1834 a cast was taken of the skull, which still bore traces of hair. In 1857 the casket was again opened, and the space around the skull filled with pitch to better preserve it – 'to be no more disturbed, we trust, till the day of doom.'

Difficulty rating:

the return of the dead:

JAMES LEGG (1801)

Three members of the Royal Academy of Art – sculptor Thomas Banks and painters Benjamin West and Richard Cosway – were of the opinion that most conventional descriptions of the Crucifixion of Christ were anatomically incorrect, with the body depicted in a variety of implausible poses. Being of an enquiring mind, the trio resolved to embark on a practical, if macabre, experiment. Through quite legitimate means they obtained the corpse of Robert Legg, an eighty-year-old Chelsea Pensioner who had murdered a colleague in his rooms. The eminent surgeon Joseph Constantine Carpue described what happened: 'A building was erected near the place of the execution; a cross provided. The subject was nailed on the cross; the cross suspended … the body, being warm, fell into the position that a dead body must fall into … When cool, a cast was made, under the direction of Mr Banks, and when the mob was dispersed it was removed to my theatre.' The corpse was then flayed (the skin removed) and the sculptor made another cast.

The first crucifixion cast, made from Legg's complete body, has been lost from sight. The flayed cast, however, is still nailed to its T-shaped cross in the Royal Academy of Arts in Piccadilly, the artwork being called *Anatomical Crucifixion (James Legg)*.

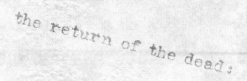

GEORGE FOSTER (1803)

In 1803, George Foster was returned to life (or the appearance of life) in a weird experiment:

He died very easy; and, after hanging the usual time, his body was cut down and conveyed to a house not far distant, where it was subjected to the galvanic process by Professor Aldini ... On the first application of the process to the face, the jaws of the deceased criminal began to quiver, and the adjoining muscles were horribly contorted, and one eye was actually opened. In the subsequent part of the process the right hand was raised and clenched, and the legs and thighs were set in motion. Mr Pass, the beadle of the Surgeons' Company, who was officially present during this experiment, was so alarmed that he died of fright soon after his return home. Some of the uninformed bystanders thought that the wretched man was on the eve of being restored to life. This, however, was impossible, as several of his friends, who were under the scaffold, had violently pulled his legs, in order to put a more speedy termination to his sufferings. The experiment, in fact, was of a better use and tendency. Its object was to show the excitability of the human frame when this animal electricity was duly applied. In cases of drowning or suffocation it promised to be of the utmost use, by reviving the action of the lungs, and thereby rekindling the expiring spark of vitality. (*The Newgate Calendar*)

HORATIO NELSON,
NATIONAL HERO
1758–1805

Height: About 5ft 6ins, taller than the legend suggests, and about average for the period. His slight build may have contributed to the sense that he was short.

Age at death: 47.

Special skills: Unrivalled seamanship, exemplary leadership, charisma, staring-into-the-face-of-death courage and a sense of his own abilities so acute that he often disobeyed orders, continuing to engage with the enemy and winning victories when more cautious opinion would have counselled retreat. Nelson was a maverick who had the knack of winning battles; while the snobs at the Admiralty may have sniffed at the clergyman's son, his men and the public loved him.

What killed him? A musket-ball fired from the French ship *Redoubtable* during the Battle of Trafalgar. Nelson had been walking the quarter-deck of HMS *Victory* during the deadly fusillade, dressed in his medals, the perfect target. The ball penetrated his spine. Dying at the moment of his greatest victory sealed the legend of Nelson the Romantic hero.

Where is he buried? St Paul's Cathedral. His state funeral was the largest of its kind until that of Queen Victoria. The coffin-plate reads, in part, 'After a series of transcendent and heroic services, this gallant admiral fell, gloriously, in the moment of brilliant and decisive Victory over the Combined Fleets of France and Spain, off Cape Trafalgar, on 21st October 1805.' An eerily lifelike wax effigy, wearing some of Nelson's own clothes, can be seen in the Undercroft Museum of Westminster Abbey.

Weaknesses and wounds: Right eye (lost at the Siege of Calvi, 1794); right arm (lost at the Battle of Santa Cruz de Tenerife, 1797); shot in the head (Battle of the Nile, 1798); injury to the abdomen (Battle of St Vincent, 1797); plus malaria, typhoid and a host of other illnesses. Bit of a half-Nelson, then.

Extra facts and zombie quotes: The *Victory* had no lead with which to make a coffin, so a large cask called a leaguer was filled with brandy to preserve the body. A week later *Victory* arrived at Gibraltar, where the barrel was topped up with spirit of wine, and the alcohol was replaced twice more on the five-week voyage to England. During this time the crew made a point of drinking the siphoned-off brandy, an episode known as 'tapping the Admiral'. At Portsmouth the body was found to be in good condition, but the bowels were removed because they had started to putrefy. At Woolwich, as it was taken out from one coffin and deposited in another, the body amazed all and sundry by being in near-perfect condition two months after death. Nelson's zombie may well have a slight hint of the distillery to it.

Difficulty rating:

JANE AUSTEN,
NATIONAL TREASURE
1775–1817

Height: She was described as 'tall and slender', which perhaps means she was about 5ft 7ins, above the average height for women of the period.

Age at death: 41.

Special skills: Writing some of the most widely read books in the world. Austen was also the first classic writer to receive a zombie parody, with Seth Grahame-Smith's *Pride and Prejudice and Zombies* (2009) rewriting the plot slightly to account for hordes of 'unmentionables' eating their way through Regency England, and turning the husband-seeking Bennett sisters into kick-ass ninjas. (N.B. She may be armed with some pretty sharp dialogue.)

What killed her? A long illness, for which several diagnoses have been suggested, ranging from tuberculosis and typhus to an endocrine disorder and lymphatic cancer.

Where is she buried? Winchester Cathedral.

Weaknesses and wounds: Other than her fatal illness, Jane was in good health.

Extra facts and zombie quotes: 'It is a truth universally acknowledged, that a single zombie in possession of a good appetite, must be in want of some brains.' Jane Austen didn't use those words exactly, but she did write the following zombie-friendly lines:

'I may have lost my heart, but not my self-control.' (*Emma*)

'I walk: I prefer walking.' *(Persuasion)*

'Life could do nothing for her, beyond giving time for a better preparation for death.' (*Sense and Sensibility*)

'I do not wish to avoid the walk. The distance is nothing when one has a motive.' (*Pride and Prejudice*)

N.B. Fancy dress is recommended for this one: Regency trousers, nice Empire-line gown, bonnet over your helmet. Ten extra points if you say, 'Mr *Darcy*!' Those of a cruel disposition might also like to add that they prefer the Brontës.

Difficulty rating:

Historical disclaimer: The publishers cannot be held responsible if the re-animated Ms Austen, rather than being a middle-class pushover, uses her sharp wit to recruit her fellow Winchester dead, including such warlike figures as Cnut (see p. 30), William II (see p. 38) and at least seven Anglo-Saxon kings. Sneaky creatures, writers.

WILLIAM BURKE,
SERIAL KILLER

1792–1829

Height: About 5ft 6ins.

Age at death: 36.

Special skills: Murder. The infamous Burke and Hare were not bodysnatchers, as is usually stated. Instead of robbing graves, they murdered people and sold the fresh bodies to the anatomists. Between them they killed at least sixteen victims, making them the most prolific serial-killing duo in British criminal history. The usual method of dispatch was suffocation, as this left no marks on the body, therefore increasing its value.

What killed him? When Burke and Hare were finally caught, there was insufficient evidence to convict; William Hare was therefore persuaded to turn King's Evidence, for which he was released without charge. Despite many rumours, no-one knows exactly what happened to him, the last definitive sighting being of him walking westwards from Dumfries towards the Stranraer ferry to his native Ireland. As for the less lucky Burke, he was hanged before a crowd of over 25,000 people. The corpse was then publically dissected, during which event the anatomist Alexander Munro dipped his quill into Burke's blood and wrote: 'This is written with the blood of Wm Burke, who was hanged at Edinburgh. This blood was taken from his head.'

Where is he buried? Following the dissection, Burke's skeleton was defleshed, preserved in salt, stored in a barrel and used in lectures. It was then articulated and put on display in the University of Edinburgh's Anatomical Museum, where, after a recent cleaning, it can still be admired today. The original label reads: 'IRISH (MALE)

WILLIAM BURKE.
FROM A
DRAWING MADE AT THE TIME

The Skeleton of WILLIAM BURKE, THE NOTORIOUS MURDERER hanged at Edinburgh, 29th January, 1829.' Sections of his skin removed during the dissection were turned into souvenirs – a wallet of his tanned skin is on display in Edinburgh's Surgeon's Hall Museum, while the Police Information Centre on the Royal Mile has a calling card case fashioned from Burke's skin. Meanwhile, his brain is in a jar in the Wellcome Collection in London.

Weaknesses and wounds: Well, all his bones are in one place...

Extra facts and zombie quotes: The Anatomical Museum also has William Hare's life mask and Burke's death mask, and next to Burke's bones hangs the articulated skeleton of John Howison, the Cramond Murderer, the last person in Britain to be both hanged and dissected.

Difficulty rating: 👁👁

the return of the dead:

THE BOG BODIES OF IRELAND
(1753 ONWARDS)

Eighty-nine preserved bodies have been found in the bogs and peat mosses of Ireland. A small sampling:

Mulkeeragh, County Derry (1753): a soldier in full tartan military uniform, laid out beneath a long tartan cloak. Both body and clothes were very well preserved. The 'Highland Soldier' was reinterred in the same spot where he had been dug out of the bog.

Flanders, County Derry (1804): a man laid out full-length a yard below the surface, his body and homespun clothes intact, except that his head had been severed and left nearby. The proximity of the body to a certain house, and the discovery of several daggers, suggested the man had been one of the many victims of a gang of eighteenth-century cut-throats headed by Neil Grooma – the former owner of the house. The body and garment were re-interred near the spot where they were found.

Charlemont, County Armagh (1816): the body of a horse soldier, possibly from the Elizabethan period. Not just his body but his clothes, spurs and armour were preserved.

Rasharkin, County Antrim (1827): a suicide from 1776, who had been buried outside consecrated ground, in a mountain bog. His body was found without any signs of decomposition.

Ballygrudden, County Derry (1831): a woman and an infant. The woman was well-preserved and her blonde hair was as fresh as in life, although the baby's flesh had disintegrated.

the return of the dead:

JEREMY BENTHAM (1832)

Bentham was a philosopher and social reformer dedicated to the creed of Utilitarianism, or 'the maximum benefit for the maximum number of people'. When he died at the grand old age of 84, he gave careful instructions in his will regarding his cadaver:

> This my will and special request I make ... to the intent and with the desire that mankind may reap some small benefit in and by my decease ... How little service soever it may have been in my power to render to mankind during my lifetime ... I shall at least be not altogether useless after my death.

Firstly, the body was publically dissected, in an attempt to remove the stigma and fear of dissection. Strips of his skin were tanned and distributed – there is an example in the Wellcome Collection in London. Then his severed head was preserved through desiccation – in the Maori fashion – and his skeleton articulated in a seated position, with a supporting iron armature bolted to Bentham's favourite chair. The skeleton was dressed in the clothes he habitually wore in life, padded out to give the illusion of a body. Unfortunately the desiccation pro-

cess went wrong, and the head was too ghastly for display. Instead, an uncannily lifelike wax face and head was substituted, the entire ensemble completed with a fine broad-brimmed hat and Bentham's favourite walking-stick, 'Dapple'. And to this day the Auto-Icon ('Self-Image') of Jeremy Bentham sits staring impassively from a glass-fronted wood-panelled box in the South Cloisters of University College London, the institution he helped found.

Bentham's rather grotesque head – complete with the glass eyes he carried around in his pocket for ten years, anticipating his death – was for many years displayed in or near the Auto-Icon. However, it was irresistible to students, and after being stolen and 'ransomed' for charity in 1975 it was securely stored, and currently resides within the Conservation Safe of the Institute of Archaeology at the College. The Auto-Icon has recently been conserved – and an infestation of insects removed – and is in excellent condition. Go and see it – it's amazing (7.30 a.m. to 6 p.m., Monday to Friday, entry free).

MARY SHELLEY,
AUTHOR
1797–1851

Height: Perhaps 5ft 2ins.

Age at death: 53.

Special skills: Writing *Frankenstein*, and hence changing the face of horror and literature for ever.

What killed her? A brain tumour.

Where is she buried? St Peter's church, Bournemouth. The Shelley family vault, beneath a large capstone in the churchyard, also includes the heart of her husband Percy Bysshe Shelley, taken from his body after he drowned off the coast of Italy.

Weaknesses and wounds: Mary suffered from ill-health for much of her life.

Extra facts and zombie quotes: Frankenstein's creature is in many ways the first zombiform monster of literature, a being re-animated from dead body parts by a mysterious spark of life. Part of the creature's genesis came from Percy Shelley's interest in the new discoveries of electricity. Mary recorded how she listened to her husband and the poet Lord Byron discuss the experiments of the natural philosopher Dr Erasmus Darwin (Charles Darwin's grandfather), who 'preserved a piece of vermicelli in a glass case till by some extraordinary means it began to move with a voluntary motion ... Perhaps a corpse would be reanimated; galvanism had given token of such things: perhaps the component parts of a creature might be manufactured, brought together, and endued with vital warmth.' When coming up with the idea, Mary wrote: 'I saw the hideous phantasm of a man stretched out, and then, on the

working of some powerful engine, show signs of life, and stir with an uneasy, half vital motion.' In the book, this is how the creature comes to life: 'With an anxiety that almost amounted to agony, I collected the instruments of life around me, that I might infuse a spark of being into the lifeless thing that lay at my feet. It was already one in the morning; the rain pattered dismally against the panes, and my candle was nearly burnt out, when by the glimmer of the half-extinguished light, I saw the dull yellow eye of the creature open; it breathed hard, and a convulsive motion agitated its limbs.' Or, as the 1931 film directed by James Whale put it, 'It's alive!'

Difficulty rating:

THE DUKE
OF WELLINGTON,
WAR COMMANDER
1769–1852

Height: About 5ft 7ins (accounts vary – but he was certainly not tall).

Age at death: 83.

Special skills: Everyone knows Wellington defeated Napoleon at the Battle of Waterloo, but brilliant field commanders do not appear out of nowhere. Arthur Wellesley learned his trade fighting in the Netherlands, India and Denmark before conducting an extraordinary six-year campaign against the French in Portugal, Spain and southern France. This Peninsular War made his reputation and his title – the first Duke of Wellington. Arthur Bryant's 1971 biography called him 'The Invincible General', which is largely accurate: as well as being a master of battlefield logistics and tactics, Wellington was also tough as old boots, surviving on little food and sleep, riding endlessly, and often leading his armies from the front. 'Old Nosey' was less able as a politician, being deeply conservative and opposed to parliamentary reform, which he saw as the victory of the rabble over their rightful rulers. Hardly anyone now remembers that he was twice a rather rubbish prime minister.

What killed him? A series of seizures following a stroke.

Where is he buried? St Paul's Cathedral. So great was his status as a national hero that he was granted a full state funeral, an honour accorded to very few. Indeed, Wellington's sarcophagus lies next to Nelson's. In 'Ode on the Death of the Duke of Wellington,' Alfred, Lord Tennyson wrote: 'Great in council and great in war / Foremost captain of his time.'

Weaknesses and wounds: Wellington fought about sixty battles, often in the thick of the combat, and his only injury was a thigh badly bruised by a spent bullet.

Extra facts and zombie quotes: At the Battle of Waterloo, Lord Uxbridge, on a horse next to Wellington, was hit by a cannonball:

Uxbridge: 'By God, sir, I've lost my leg!'

Wellington: 'By God, sir, so you have!'

Also famous for saying, at the same battle: 'Go get him, Sharpey!' (Possibly.)

Difficulty rating: 👁👁👁

Historical disclaimer: Wellington is easily one of the greatest military commanders of all time. Will St Paul's be your Waterloo?

CHARLOTTE BRONTË,
AUTHOR
1816–1855

Height: 4ft 9in or 4ft 10in.

Age at death: 38.

Special skills: Strong-minded, determined and intelligent. Although small in stature, frail and modest, Charlotte broke the mould of nineteenth-century femininity in her life and (especially) in her art. Her novel *Jane Eyre*, written under a genderless pseudonym, channelled her frustrations at the way women were forced to live their lives, and has become a classic of English literature. At a time when most genteel women were regarded as little more than ornaments or brood mares, Charlotte Brontë was free-thinking, erudite and spirited, as was her heroine Jane, who famously declared: 'I am no bird; and no net ensnares me: I am a free human being with an independent will.'

What killed her? Illness, possibly typhus, tuberculosis or pneumonia, or perhaps dehydration brought on by severe morning sickness. Her unborn child died with her.

Where is she buried? The Brontë family vault in the church of St Michael and All Angels at Haworth, Yorkshire. An inscribed pillar marks the spot.

Weaknesses and wounds: Charlotte was physically frail – her father initially refused to allow her marriage because he feared she would not survive pregnancy.

Extra facts and zombie quotes: *Jane Eyre* is a quasi-Gothic novel filled with zombie-friendly quotes:

I feel monotony and death to be almost the same.

I must keep in good health and not die.

You — you strange — you almost unearthly thing!

The final word belongs to the admirable Charlotte, from one of her letters:

But life is a battle: may we all be enabled to fight it well!

Difficulty rating:

Historical disclaimer: Just because there's a zombie apocalypse, doesn't mean Ms Brontë will do what every other zombie does and go on a rampage; she may just decide to stay in her tomb, and if that's the case there's nothing you can do to change her mind.

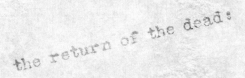

the return of the dead:

CATHERINE EARNSHAW (1847)

Wuthering Heights, the novel by Charlotte Brontë's sister Emily, contains a notorious scene where the hero-villain, Heathcliff, revisits the grave of Catherine Earnshaw, his lover who had died eighteen years previously, and finds that her corpse has been preserved:

> I got the sexton, who was digging Linton's grave, to remove the earth off her coffin lid, and I opened it. I thought, once, I would have stayed there: when I saw her face again — it is hers yet! — he had hard work to stir me; but he said it would change if the air blew on it.
>
> 'You were very wicked, Mr Heathcliff!' I exclaimed; 'were you not ashamed to disturb the dead?'
>
> 'I disturbed nobody, Nelly,' he replied; 'and I gave some ease to myself. I shall be a great deal more comfortable now; and you'll have a better chance of keeping me underground, when I get there.'

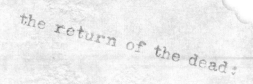

THE ROMAN FROM RIPON (1850)

The body of a man – evidently an ancient Roman – which the peat had
tanned, dried and preserved in a remarkable manner … The robes were
quite perfect and the material tough – having been tanned and preserved
by some natural agency. The toga was of a green colour, and some of the
dress of scarlet material; the stockings of a yellow cloth, and the sandals cut
out in a beautiful shape.

So wrote Thomas C. Heslington in a paper presented to the Scientific
Society of Ripon in 1867. The (reeking) body had been uncovered
during peat digging on Grewelthorpe Moor in North Yorkshire. Sadly
most of the body disintegrated on exposure to the air and whatever was
left was interred in the churchyard of Kirkby Malzeard. This unique
find has prompted some scepticism regarding the 'Roman' identifica-
tion, but analysis of the sole remaining relic – part of a shoe – shows
that it is indeed of the kind typically worn by a Romanised civilian
during the second to fourth centuries AD.

ISAMBARD KINGDOM BRUNEL,

ENGINEER

1806–1859

Height: Just over 5ft. He habitually wore his famous stovepipe hats to make himself look taller.

Age at death: 53.

Special skills: Engineering the Victorian world. You've probably used bridges, tunnels, docks, railway lines and stations (such as Paddington) that were designed and built by Brunel. His ships the SS *Great Western*, SS *Great Britain* and SS *Great Eastern* were each the largest and most innovative ships in the world at the time of their construction. Brunel also responded to a plea by Florence Nightingale (see p. 168) and designed from scratch the world's first flat-pack hospital for use in the Crimea. Brunel was a technical genius and a visionary; he changed the face of Britain. And had the best name ever.

What killed him? A stroke, probably brought on by overwork and smoking forty cigars a day.

Where is he buried? Kensal Green Cemetery, London.

Weaknesses and wounds: Brunel was almost killed while working on the Thames Tunnel, and was also injured in an incident on the *Great Britain*. But this was a man who worked eighteen hours a day at a pace that exhausted his subordinates.

Extra facts and zombie quotes: There's a good chance you'll find a precisely engineered tunnel leading from the grave. Where does it lead? You'll have to venture into the dark and find out. Oh, hello there, Mr Brunel...

Difficulty rating: 🧟

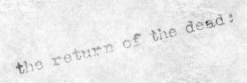

the return of the dead:

AMELIA HINKS (1858)

In a case well-documented within the pages of the medical journal *The Lancet*, the 12-year-old from Nuneaton, to all intents and purposes, died at 3.30 a.m.

> She was washed, and attired in clean linen, the jaw was tied by a white handkerchief, penny-pieces laid over her eyes, her hands, semi-clenched, placed by her side, and her feet tied together by a piece of tape. She was then carried into another room, laid on a sofa, and covered over with a sheet. She appeared stiff and cold, two large books were placed on her feet, and I have no doubt she was considered to be a sweet corpse.

At 9 a.m. Amelia's grandfather noticed a flicker of an eyelid. At 10.30 a doctor confirmed she still had a weak heartbeat. The girl eventually recovered, and claimed she had been able to hear all that was going on around her while she was being prepared for the grave.

In 1905 William Tebb and E.P. Vollum published *Premature Burial, and How It May Be Prevented*, which listed 161 examples of people being buried, dissected or even embalmed while still alive, with 222 cases where individuals narrowly escaped a similar fate.

the return of the dead:

MUMMIES IN MUSEUMS

Several British museums have excellent collections of mummies, foremost of which is the British Museum, which owns a whopping seventy-eight Egyptian mummies and thirteen South American mummies (this does mean, of course, that, come the apocalypse, the BM is going to be zombie-mummy central).

The other mummy collections are in:

Liverpool Museum: eighteen complete mummies, plus numerous other body parts and lots of animals, from cats to crocodiles.

Manchester Museum: seventeen human and thirty-one animal mummies.

The Ashmolean Museum, Oxford: eight complete mummies, one head, and a great many mummified animals.

The Wellcome Collection, London: one Peruvian mummy.

CHARLES DICKENS,
AUTHOR
1812–1870

Height: About 5ft 8ins.

Age at death: 58.

Special skills: One of the greatest novelists of all time, social critic, self-educated genius. 'Nuff said.

What killed him? A stroke.

Where is he buried? Poets' Corner, Westminster Abbey.

Weaknesses and wounds: Dickens drove himself into the ground with his superhuman workload. He was also badly affected, both psychologically and physically, by being involved in a train crash in 1865.

Extra facts and zombie quotes:

'It is required of every man,' the ghost returned, 'that the spirit within him should walk abroad among his fellow-men, and travel far and wide; and, if that spirit goes not forth in life, it is condemned to do so after death.' (*A Christmas Carol*)

'So much life in the city ran into death according to rule, time and tide waited for no man.' (*A Tale of Two Cities*)

'Death doesn't change us more than life.' (*The Old Curiosity Shop*)

Difficulty rating:

Historical disclaimer: Dickens was a workaholic; it may just be that, instead of rampaging around the streets, he may instead reach for a pen, perhaps intending to work on:

The Death and Adventures of Nicholas Nickleby

Zombey and Son

The Mystery of Edwin Dread

David Potter's Field

Really Bleak House

A Christmas Cadaver

A Tale of Two Carcasses

Great Exhumations

The Old Curiosity Corpse

CHARLES BABBAGE,
FATHER OF THE COMPUTER
1791–1871

Height: About 5ft 10ins.

Age at death: 79.

Special skills: Mathematics, inventing, codebreaking and – especially – designing the world's first computers. The Difference Engine was a mechanical device which could perform mathematical calculations, while the more complex Analytical Engine used punched cards to deliver the instructions, with a memory unit to store numbers. Neither was built during Babbage's lifetime; the idea that they could have been provides the basis for much of steampunk's generic imagining of a technologically advanced Victorian Britain.

What killed him? Renal failure.

Where is he buried? Kensal Green Cemetery, London, with a very simple plinth.

Weaknesses and wounds: Babbage was an intellectual with a comfortable lifestyle, so he might be thought of as something of a pushover, zombie-wise. But he also invented the 'pilot', the metal cow-catcher that sat at the front of steam locomotives, so give him a bit of time and a decent workshop and he'll be charging you down with some kind of armoured steam-driven device.

Extra facts and zombie quotes: Babbage bequeathed his own brain to science. Babbage's son Henry wrote: 'I have no objection ... to the idea of preserving the brain ... the brain should be known as his, and disposed of in any manner which you consider most conducive to the advancement of human knowledge and the good of the human race.'

Difficulty rating:

Historical disclaimer: Zombies and brains: it's the age-old question. Can a corpse with a missing head or brain re-animate? Babbage might provide a textbook answer, as half his remarkable brain is on display in the London Science Museum, while the other half resides in the capital's Hunterian Museum. And his body is in a cemetery several miles away from both. Will you and your compatriots need to stake out all three locations? Only you can decide.

CHARLES DARWIN,
SCIENTIST
1809–1882

Height: 6ft.

Age at death: 71.

Special skills: Changing the world forever. His books *On the Origin of Species* and *The Descent of Man* introduced the idea of evolution through natural selection and the then-shocking concept that humans were descended from ape-like ancestors. Merely mentioning his name will still cause apoplexy amongst conservative religious Americans. Well done, Charles.

What killed him? Heart disease.

Where is he buried? Westminster Abbey, close to Sir Isaac Newton (see p. 114)

Weaknesses and wounds: Darwin suffered chronic ill-health for much of his adult life. However, during his five-year voyage around the world aboard HMS *Beagle,* he vigorously walked and rode across all kinds of difficult terrains, from jungles to mountains, enthusiastically collecting zoological and botanical specimens.

Extra facts and zombie quotes: Darwin initially intended to study medicine, but the sight of blood made him queasy; how will he react to the appetites of zombiehood? Perhaps more intriguingly, how will the 'Father of Evolution' respond to the rise of what might be seen as the next stage in the evolving human story? Will he be taking notes on a new theory while simultaneously trying to eat your brain?

Deathbed quote: 'I am not the least afraid of death.'

Difficulty rating: 😵😵

Historical disclaimer: Charles Darwin is smarter than you. His zombie may be too; expect the unexpected.

KARL MARX,
PHILOSOPHER
1818–1883

Height: Probably about 5ft 8ins.

Age at death: 64.

Special skills: Innovative political and economic analysis. Marx is easily one of the most influential people of the past 200 years. He's also probably been turning in his grave at the brutal antics of those who professed to follow his ideas, such as Stalin, Mao and the Khmer Rouge.

What killed him? Bronchitis and pleurisy.

Where is he buried? Highgate Cemetery, London. His original, extremely modest gravemarker was replaced in 1954 by a tall plinth topped by a huge bust of the bearded philosopher, who appears not dissimilar to conceptions of the God of the Old Testament. The aggrandisement was paid for by the Communist Party of Great Britain, and was sufficiently robust to survive a bomb attack in 1970. The monument cannot be missed, and makes a useful marker if you are staking out any of Highgate's other celebrity inhabitants, such as George Eliot, Michael Faraday or Malcolm McLaren, not to mention a vampire that supposedly hung round the cemetery in the 1970s.

Weaknesses and wounds: Poor living conditions and bereavement contributed to a decline in health over many months. Avoided military service as a young man because of his 'weak chest'.

Extra facts and zombie quotes: In his masterwork, *Capital,* Marx wrote: 'Capital is dead labour, which, vampire-like, lives only by sucking living labour, and lives the more, the more labour it sucks'.

Difficulty rating:

Historical disclaimer: If you are tempted to see the rise of zombies in popular culture as a metaphor for the revenge of the poor and dispossessed, then perhaps, come the apocalypse, the re-animated hordes will find some kind of saviour in the bolshie sage of Highgate: 'Zombies of the world unite; you have nothing to lose but your brains.'

JACK THE RIPPER,
POPULAR LETTER WRITER

?~?

Height: Unknown, although some witnesses described a man between 5ft 5ins and 5ft 7ins tall.

Age at death: Unknown.

Special skills: Handy with a knife and (possibly) surgical instruments. Murderous, frenzied rage directed specifically at lower-class women, with at least five victims in the terrible autumn of 1888. Bit of a bad 'un, all in all.

What killed him? Unknown.

Where is he buried? Unknown. Of all the returning corpses in this book, this is the one with a million-in-one chance to locate. Jack's enduring fame is not due to the number of his murders or the vile nature of his mutilations, but because (a) he was the first serial killer celebrated within the pages of the new mass-market newspapers, and (b) he was never caught or even identified. To this day the enigma of his identity continues to fuel a never-ending industry devoted to solving the mystery. While even worse murderers are long forgotten, Jack – or whatever his name was – remains as the faceless patron of serial-killer culture.

Weaknesses and wounds: Unknown – though the first should probably include English grammar (see below).

Extra facts and zombie quotes: Jack liked opening up the human body and rummaging around inside; in one of his letters (which may be hoaxes) he even admitted to cannibalism ('I send you half the Kidne I took from one women prasarved it for you tother piece I fried and ate it was very nise'). One of the other Ripper let-

ters finished off: 'My knife's so nice and sharp I want to get to work right away if I get a chance. Good Luck.' You get the feeling Saucy Jack would positively welcome the zombie apocalypse.

Difficulty rating: 👹👹

Historical disclaimer: At least thirty men have been suggested as the Ripper, none of them convincingly, so it's probably not worth planning a Ripper-offing day out. However, if you do happen to hear of a zombie wandering around Whitechapel with a big knife, well...

LEWIS CARROLL,
AUTHOR
1832–1898

Height: About 5ft 11ins, potions allowing. ('I'm afraid I can't put it more clearly,' Alice replied very politely, 'for I can't understand it myself, to begin with; and being so many different sizes in a day is very confusing.')

Age at death: 65.

Special skills: Writing nonsense. ('Why, sometimes I've believed as many as six impossible things before breakfast.')

What killed him? Pneumonia.

Where is he buried? Mount Cemetery, Guildford.

Weaknesses and wounds: Carroll suffered from migraines, lung problems and a stammer for much of his life.

Extra facts and zombie quotes: In real life Lewis Carroll was the pen-name of Charles Lutwidge Dodgson, a mild-mannered Victorian eccentric whose immortal creations *Alice's Adventures in Wonderland* and *Through the Looking Glass* are goldmines for zombie quotes. Carroll had some good advice on dealing with zombies, for example:

> The Queen had only one way of settling all difficulties, great or small. 'Off with his head!' she said without even looking around.

> She waited for a few minutes to see if she was going to shrink any further: she felt a little nervous about this; 'for it might end, you know,' said Alice to herself, 'in my going out altogether, like a candle. I wonder what I should be like then?'

'What does it matter where my body happens to be?' he said. 'My mind goes on working all the same.'

Difficulty rating:

Historical disclaimer: Don't be surprised if the re-animated Carroll is accompanied by a psychedelic phantasmagoria of bizarre creatures. The White Rabbit, Mad Hatter and Caterpillar shouldn't pose too many problems, but if the Jabberwocky turns up, make sure you have your vorpal sword to hand.

OSCAR WILDE,
AUTHOR
1854–1900

Height: 6ft 3ins.

Age at death: 46.

Special skills: Wit, aestheticism, writing some of the best-loved plays ever performed in English, creating the enduringly resonant *The Picture of Dorian Gray*, and generally being a bit of a clever clogs. Wilde's artistic triumphs were annihilated when he was prosecuted for his homosexual double life and spent two years in jail. As soon as he was released he left for France, where he spent the final three years of his life in artistic decline and financial turpitude. A month before his death he said to a friend, 'My wallpaper and I are fighting a duel to the death. One or the other of us has to go.'

'I dreamt I was supping with the dead,' he said to Reggie Turner. 'My dear Oscar,' replied Turner, 'you were probably the life and soul of the party.'

What killed him? Meningitis.

Where is he buried? In Wilde's comedy *The Importance of Being Ernest*, Jack, speaking of his supposedly deceased brother, says, 'He seems to have expressed a desire to be buried in Paris.' To which the Revd Dr Chasuble replies, 'I fear that hardly points to any very serious state of mind at the last.' Wilde was laid to rest in Bagneux Cemetery, outside Paris. The funeral was a 'sixth class' affair, with a cheap coffin and a shabby hearse, a reflection of Wilde's debt-ridden last years. In 1909 the remains were moved to the more distinguished Père Lachaise burial ground within the city, and a grand monument by the sculptor Jacob Epstein erected over them.

Weaknesses and wounds: Wilde suffered badly in jail, rupturing an eardrum and collapsing from malnutrition and illness. His health never recovered.

Extra facts and zombie quotes:

> 'Yes, death. Death must be so beautiful. To lie in the soft brown earth, with the grasses waving above one's head, and listen to silence. To have no yesterday, and no tomorrow. To forget time, to forgive life, to be at peace.' (*The Canterville Ghost*)

Difficulty rating:

Historical disclaimer: If, instead of a rotting corpse, you find Oscar in the pink of health and clutching a suspiciously decayed painting under his arm, well, don't blame us.

QUEEN VICTORIA,
EMPRESS
1819–1901

Height: Victoria was 5ft 2in in her youth, but she lost about 3ins in old age – wear a pair of greaves and you should be fine.

Age at death: 81.

Special skills: Perseverance. Not being amused. Robustness: she outlived the prime ministers and foreign secretaries with whom she clashed, survived numerous amateurish assassination attempts, and by the end of her reign she was almost universally beloved. The British love old codgers, and by her Diamond Jubilee in 1897 Victoria was the greatest old codger the country has ever seen. Queen for an incredible sixty-three years, she had lived and reigned for so long that, when she died, no-one in the court or government had any experience of what to do when a monarch passed away.

What killed her? Basically, old age – she survived being shot at (three times), a man breaking into Bucks Palace to see her (four times), being shot at again (this time by a hunchback), shot at again by a man who forgot to load his gun, a painful strike on the head with a cane that 'crushed her bonnet', a man who tried to hold her at gunpoint (again, no bullet), and another attempt to shoot her at Windsor Station.

Where is she buried? The massive Royal Mausoleum in Frogmore Estate, adjoining Windsor Castle. She is buried with her husband, Prince Albert, who predeceased her by twenty-nine years. Many princes and princesses are interred in the surrounding Royal Burial Ground, including the king-abdicatee, Edward VIII.

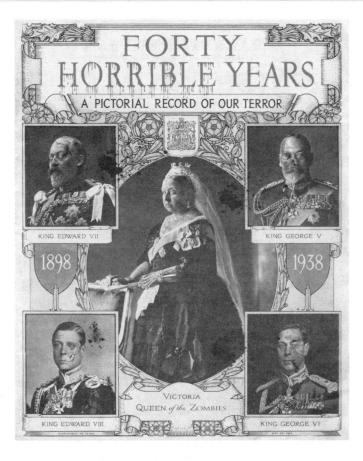

Weaknesses and wounds: Despite a few illnesses here and there, and being overweight, Victoria had the constitution of an ox.

Extra facts and zombie quotes: This is the woman who sternly said, 'We are not interested in the possibilities of defeat. They do not exist.' She also caught one would-be assassin by deliberately driving the same way after a failed attempt to kill her in order to tempt him into trying again. Tread cautiously.

Difficulty rating:

FLORENCE NIGHTINGALE,

FOUNDER OF MODERN NURSING

1820–1910

Height: She was often described as 'tall', but we don't know her exact height.

Age at death: 90.

Special skills: A strong stomach – a *really* strong stomach. Taking on the British Establishment and winning. It's hard to imagine now just how awful medical care was in the early nineteenth century, especially in the military. During the Crimean War Florence headed a task force of nurses set up to improve conditions of care for wounded soldiers. Immortalised as 'the Lady with the Lamp', she accidentally became a national heroine. After the war the steely Florence spent a lifetime arguing against the entrenched conservative ideas of men in power. Her greatest achievements were changing the face of nursing so that it became a respectable profession for women, setting out the rules of nursing care and sanitation, and training nurses who went out into the wider world – from the British Empire to Japan and the USA. It is arguable that in Victorian Britain she was the most influential woman after Queen Victoria herself. Respect.

What killed her? Basically, old age.

Where is she buried? St Margaret churchyard, East Wellow, Hampshire. Her funeral service was held in St Paul's Cathedral but her family declined the offer of burial in Westminster Abbey, as being contrary to Florence's wishes for a modest memorial. Only her initials, FN, appear on her gravestone.

Weaknesses and wounds: Florence was often confined to bed by a viral infection called brucellosis, which make sufferers sweat profusely. Suffered sporadically from depression. Completely blind in the last years of her life.

Extra facts and zombie quotes: In recent years her reputation has taken a bit of a drubbing from some historians, who have pointed out that perhaps she wasn't as effective a reformer has been made out. It would be amusing if said historians could be brought to confront the re-animated Florence, as there might be a robust exchange of views: this was a woman who browbeat generals and government ministers.

Difficulty rating:

W.G. GRACE,
CRICKETER
1848–1915

Height: 6ft 2ins, with a build to match.

Age at death: 67.

Special skills: William Gilbert Grace, a big man with a big beard, was the most recognisable man of his era. He was a cricketing phenomenon, excelling at all aspects of the sport, but especially batting. A qualified medical doctor, his team was Gloucestershire, and he also played for and captained England. Over a career lasting forty-three years, he scored 54,896 first-class runs, including 126 centuries, and took 2,876 wickets. Well played, that chap.

What killed him? A heart attack. When he died there was a national outpouring of grief that temporarily eclipsed the horrors of the First World War.

Where is he buried? Beckenham Cemetery, Bromley, London, in the family plot. A plinth bearing a bat, ball and wickets simply reads: 'W.G. Grace, Doctor and Cricketer.'

Weaknesses and wounds: Grace was still playing cricket and scoring centuries well into his 60s.

Extra facts and zombie quotes: As well as owning one of the Great Beards of History, he was a sporting powerhouse who could send a ball much farther than you can. All he has to do is pick up something vaguely cricket bat-shaped (say, a femur), find something vaguely ball-shaped (say, a neighbour's skull) – and you're out, mate.

Difficulty rating: 👀

T.E. LAWRENCE,
'LAWRENCE OF ARABIA'

1888–1935

Height: 5ft 5ins.

Age at death: 46.

Special skills: Lawrence went from an able but obscure field archaeologist specialising in the Middle East to the British Empire's most valued asset in the fight against Ottoman Turkey during the First World War. He organised, motivated and led disaffected Arab tribes, adopted Arab dress, became the confidante of princes, and endured extreme conditions with a tenacious disregard for his own comfort. To get a sense of his personality, consider this commemorative quote from Winston Churchill in 1936:

> The world looks with some awe upon a man who appears unconcernedly indifferent to home, money, comfort, rank, or even power and fame. The world feels not without a certain apprehension, that here is someone outside its jurisdiction; someone before whom its allurements may be spread in vain; someone strangely enfranchised, untamed, untrammelled by convention, moving independent of the ordinary currents of human action.

Complex, volatile, inspirational, enigmatic and austere, Lawrence was above all *tough*. He was an expert climber, so you might want to look up occasionally. Similarly expert on English castles and siege warfare – so if you hole up in a castle, he *will* still get you.

What killed him? Two boys on bicycles. They were hidden in a dip in the road as Lawrence was returning on his motorbike from sending a telegram at Bovington post office. He swerved to avoid them and crashed. He died six days later from head injuries. The restored Brough Superior motorcycle is in the Imperial War Museum, London.

Where is he buried? In a clearly marked grave in the second (overflow) cemetery at St Nicholas church, Moreton, Dorset. There are two worn memorial stones at the carpark close to the spot where he was killed, on the minor road between Wool and his tiny cottage at Cloud's Hill (now owned by the National Trust). You can also admire a full-length marble effigy of him in Arab dress in St Martin's church, Wareham, Dorset.

Weaknesses and wounds:
As well as his fatal injuries, Lawrence had many years earlier broken a shoulder blade and two ribs during a plane crash. Also suffered from malaria.

Extra facts and zombie quotes: Lawrence was a superb writer. *The Seven Pillars of Wisdom,* a combined account of the Arab Revolt and his own spiritual journey, is a masterpiece. In a later book, *The Mint,* he wrote: 'Many men would take the death-sentence without a whimper, to escape the life-sentence which fate carries in her other hand.'

Difficulty rating:

the return of the dead:

SOME RECENT REVENANTS:
THE MAN FROM BURWELL FEN (1850s?)

Most shudderingly entrancing of all was the Ancient Briton, who suddenly emerged from the peat in Burwell Fen, when the turf-diggers were at work. He stood upright in his dug-out canoe. His lank black hair dropped to his shoulders. The peat-dark skin was still stretched over the bones of his face. The eyes had gone but the eye-sockets were dark with mystery. He was clad in a long leather jacket, belted, with garters round his legs and the right arm was raised as though about to cast a spear. That body of the unknown hunter, the nameless warrior, had been preserved in the peat for uncounted aeons of time.

So did James Wentworth Day describe the finding of a bog body near Newmarket, Cambridgeshire, in the 1970 edition of his book *The History of the Fens*. Unfortunately for us, the body apparently 'crumbled to dust in the sharp Fen air.'

The details about standing upright in the canoe and the man's raised arm make me suspect a hoax, as there is no date, no precise location, and no corroborating evidence.

ANTHONY DE LUCY (1981)

A coffin uncovered at St Bees Priory, Cumbria, turned out to hold not the skeleton of a monk but the remarkably well-preserved body of a medieval knight.

His body had been enshrouded, covered in beeswax and wrapped in a lead sheet within a wooden coffin. The combination had excluded the usual agents of decay. An autopsy was quickly held, during which all the organs were found healthy and intact, while liquid blood poured out from an injury to the lungs. It was as if he had died just a few days earlier. Hair, eyes (including retinas), genitals and skin were complete, although exposure to the air quickly brought about changes. The body was reburied at St Bees, and further research has identified the individual as Anthony de Lucy, who died at the age of about 40 in 1368, fighting on a Crusade against the pagan Lithuanians.

LINDOW MAN (1983)

Originally known as 'Pete Bog', the preserved body of this Iron Age man caused a media sensation when it emerged from the Cheshire peat. He was a victim of a ritualistic 'triple death' – blunt force trauma to the head, garrotted and then had his throat cut – and was clearly a human sacrifice, possibly connected with Druidic religion. Lindow Man now sits under glass in the British Museum – go and visit him. Worsley Man – another human sacrifice from the same period, whose head was all that was preserved – was found in 1958 and is now in Manchester Museum.

LINDOW WOMAN (1983)

When a preserved female head turned up in the bog of Lindow Moss, the police thought it was that of Malika Reyn-Bardt, who went missing in 1961. They had always suspected her estranged husband of the murder, and when confronted with the head, Peter Reyn-Bardt confessed to chopping his wife's body up with an axe twenty-two years earlier, and throwing the remains into the Moss.

Subsequent examination showed that the head dated from the third century AD. The remains of Malika Reyn-Bardt have never been found.

AND FINALLY...

In November 2012 Sam Ledward of Gwernaffield, Flintshire, celebrated his 106th birthday, which is not bad going considering he was declared dead in 1936. He fell into a coma following a motorcycle accident, and only revived as he was being wheeled to the mortuary.

BIBLIOGRAPHY

Anon., *The Chapter House, The Pyx Chamber and Treasury, The Undercroft Museum* (Dean and Chapter of Westminster; London, n.d.)

Aitchison, Nick, *Macbeth Man and Myth* (Sutton Publishing; Stroud, 1999)

Alderman, Clifford Lindsey, *Blood-Red the Roses: the Wars of the Roses* (Bailey Brothers and Swinfen; Folkestone, 1973)

Arnold, Ken & Danielle Olsen (eds), *Medicine Man: The Forgotten Museum of Henry Wellcome* (British Museum Press; London, 2011)

Asher, Michael, *Lawrence: The Uncrowned King of Arabia* (Viking; London, 1998)

Bakewell, Michael, *Lewis Carroll: A Biography* (Heinemann; London, 1996)

Barber, Paul, *Vampires, Burial and Death: Folklore and Reality* (Yale University Press; New Haven and London, 1988)

Barber, Richard, *Living Legends* (British Broadcasting Corporation; London, 1980)

Barker, Felix, and John Gay, *Highgate Cemetery: Victorian Valhalla* (John Murray; London, 1984)

Barlow, Frank, *William Rufus* (University of California Press; Berkeley and Los Angeles, 1983)

Barrow, Geoffrey W.S., *Robert Bruce & The Community of the Realm of Scotland* (Edinburgh University Press; Edinburgh, 1988 [1965])

Robert Bartlett, *England Under the Norman and Angevin Kings 1075-1225* (Oxford University Press; Oxford, 2000)

Bates, David, *William the Conqueror* (George Philip; London, 1989)

Bevan, Bryan, *Nell Gwyn* (Robert Hale; London, 1969)

Bingham, Caroline, *The Life and Times of Edward II* (Book Club Associates; London, 1973)

Bingham, Caroline, *Robert the Bruce* (Constable; London, 1998)

Bondeson, Jan, *Buried Alive: the terrifying history of our most primal fear* (W.W. Norton; New York & London, 2001)

Boswell, James, *The Life of Samuel Johnson* (Penguin; Harmondsworth, 1979)

Brewer, Clifford, *The Death of Kings: a medical history of the Kings and Queens of England* (Abson; London, 2000)

Brier, Bob, *The Encyclopedia of Mummies* (Checkmark Books; New York, 1998)

Briggs, Katherine M., 'Historical Traditions in English Folk-Tales' in *Folklore* Vol.75, No.4 (1964)

Brothwell, Don, *The Bog Man and the Archaeology of People* (British Museum; London, 1986)

Bryant, Arthur, *The Great Duke* (History Book Club; London, 1971)

Cantor, Norman F. (ed.), *The Pimlico Encyclopedia of the Middle Ages* (Pimlico; London, 1999)

Carver, Martin, *Sutton Hoo: Burial Ground of Kings?* (British Museum Publications; London, 1998)

Collingridge, Vanessa, *Boudica* (Ebury Press; London, 2005)

Connolly, S.J. (ed.), *The Oxford Companion to Irish History* (Oxford University Press; Oxford, 1998)

Craig, R., 'Alfred the Great: a diagnosis' in *Journal of the Royal Society of Medicine,* Vol.84 (May 1991)

Davidson, H.R. Ellis, 'Folklore and Man's Past' in *Folklore*, Vol.74, No.4 (1963)

Defoe, Daniel, *A Journal of the Plague Year* (Everyman; London, 1962 [1722])

Earle, Peter, *The Pirate Wars* (Methuen; London, 2003)

Edwards, Owen Dudley, *Burke & Hare* (The Mercat Press; Edinburgh, 1993)

Ellmann, Richard, *Oscar Wilde* (Penguin; London, 1988)

Fraser, Antonia (ed.), *The Lives of the Kings & Queens of England* (Book Club Associates; London, 1975)

Geoffrey of Burton (ed. R. Bartlett), *Life and Miracles of St Modwenna* (Clarendon Press; Oxford, 2002)

Goulding, Christopher, 'The real Doctor Frankenstein?' in *Journal of the Royal Society of Medicine* Vol.95 No.5 (May 2002)

Graham, Roderick, *An Accidental Tragedy: The life of Mary, Queen of Scots* (Birlinn; Edinburgh, 2008)

Grainge, William *et al, Ripon Millenary, a record of the festival. Also a history of the city, arranged under its wakemen and mayors from the year 1400* (W. Harrison; Ripon, 1892)

Greenwood, Douglas, *Who's buried where in England* (Constable; London, 1982)

Grinnell-Milne, Duncan, *The Killing of William Rufus* (David & Charles; Newton Abbott, 1968)

Haining, Peter, *The English Highwayman: A legend unmasked* (Robert Hale; London, 1981)

Hibbert, Christopher, *Nelson: a personal history* (Viking; London, 1994)

Hibbert, Christopher, *Queen Victoria: a personal history* (HarperCollins; London, 2000)

Hoffmann, Ann, *Lives of the Tudor Age 1485-1603* (Osprey; London, 1977)

Kerrigan, Michael, *Who Lies Where – a guide to famous graves* (Fourth Estate; London, 1995)

Keyworth, G. David, 'Was the Vampire of the Eighteenth Century a unique type of Undead-corpse?' in *Folklore* Vol.117, No.3 (Dec., 2006)

Kightly, Charles, *Folk Heroes of Britain* (Thames & Hudson; London, 1982)

Lacey, Robert, *The Life and Times of Henry VIII* (Book Club Associates; London, 1972)

Lane, Brian, *The Encyclopedia of Cruel and Unusual Punishment* (True Crime; London, 1993)

Lane, Margaret, *Samuel Johnson and his World* (Hamish Hamilton; London, 1975)

Lewis, Jayne Elizabeth, *Mary Queen of Scots: Romance and Nation* (Routledge; London and New York, 1998)

Lewis, Samuel, *A Topographical Dictionary of Ireland* (S. Lewis & Co.; London, 1837)

McDowall, William, *History of Dumfries* (Adam & Charles Black; Edinburgh, 1867)

Mankowitz, Wolf, *Dickens of London* (MacMillan; New York, 1977)

Marmoy, C.F.A., 'The 'Auto-Icon of Jeremy Bentham at University College London' in *Medical History,* Vol.2 (1958)

Maxwell, H. (ed.), *Chronicle of Lanercost, 1272-1346* (James Maclehose and Sons; Glasgow, 1913)

Merrifield, Ralph, *The Archaeology of Ritual and Magic* (B.T. Batsford; London, 1987)

Newark, Peter, *The Crimson Book of Highwaymen* (Jupiter Books; London, 1979)

Normington, Susan, *Napoleon's Children* (Alan Sutton Publishing; Stroud, 1993)

Parker, T.M., *The English Reformation to 1558* (Oxford University Press; Oxford, 1966)

Parker Pearson, Mike *et al,* 'Evidence for mummification in Bronze Age Britain' in *Antiquity,* Vol.79, No.305 (2005)

Parker Pearson, Mike *et al,* 'Further evidence for mummification in Bronze Age Britain' in *Antiquity,* Vol.81, No.312 (September 2007)

Posel, Deborah, & Pamila Gupta, 'The Life of the Corpse: Framing Reflections and Questions' in *African Studies*, Vol.68, No.3 (2009)

Prescott, H.F.M., *Mary Tudor: The Spanish Tudor* (Phoenix; London, 2003 [1940])

Rayner, J.L., and G.T Crook (eds), *The Complete Newgate Calendar* 5 vols, (Navarre Society; London, 1926)

Reynolds, A., 'Executions and Hard Anglo-Saxon Justice' in *British Archaeology* Vol.31 (February 1998)

Reynolds, Lucy, Sam & Andrew (eds), *Burial in Early Medieval England and Wales* (The Society for Medieval Archaeology; London, 2002)

Richardson, Ruth, *Death, Dissection and the Destitute* (Penguin; London, 1989)

Richardson, Ruth, and Brian Hurwitz, 'Jeremy Bentham's Self Image: An Exemplary Bequest For Dissection' in *The British Medical Journal* Vol.295, 18 July 1987

Rival, Paul, *The Six Wives of Henry VIII* (Heinemann; London, 1971 [1937])

Roberts, Charlotte A., *Human Remains in Archaeology: A Handbook* (Council for British Archaeology; York, 2009)

Robinson, Tony, *In Search of British Heroes* (Boxtree; London, 2004)

Roden, Christopher and Barbara Roden, 'Twelve Medieval Ghost Stories' in *M. R. James, A Pleasing Terror: The Complete Supernatural Writings*, ed. C. Roden and B. Roden (Ash-Tree Press; Ashcroft, British Columbia, 2001)

Roughhead, William, *Notable British Trials: Burke and Hare* (William Hodge & Co.; London, Edinburgh & Glasgow, 1921)

Sawyer, Peter (ed.), *The Oxford Illustrated History of the Vikings* (Oxford University Press; Oxford, 1997)

Schama, Simon, *A History of Britain* 3 vols, (BBC Worldwide; London, 2000)

Simpson, Jacqueline, 'Repentant soul or walking corpse? Debatable apparitions in medieval England' in *Folklore*, Vol.114, No.3 (2003)

Stead, I.M., J.B. Bourke & Don Brothwell, *Lindow Man: The Body in the Bog* (Guild Publishing; London, 1986)

Stevenson, J., *The History of William of Newburgh* (Llanerch Publishers; Felinfach, 1996 [1856])

Summers, Montague, *The Vampire* (Senate; London, 1995 [1928])

Sunstein, Emily W., *Mary Shelley: Romance and Reality* (The Johns Hopkins University Press; Baltimore, 1991)

Suzuki, Mihoko (ed.), *The History of British Women's Writing, 1610-1690* (Palgrave Macmillan; London, 2011)

Taylor, Alison, *Burial Practice in Early England* (Tempus; Stroud, 2001)

Taylor, Joseph, *The danger of premature interment* (Simpkin & Marshall; London, 1816)

Tebb, William, and Edward Perry Vollum, *Premature Burial, and how it may be prevented* (Swan Sonnenschein & Co.; London, 1896)

Thomas, Keith, *Religion and the Decline of Magic* (Penguin; Harmondsworth, 1982 [1971])

Thompson, Victoria Jane, *The Understanding of Death in England 800-1100* (Doctoral thesis, University of York, May 2000)

Turner, R.C.,M. Rhodes and J.P. Wild, 'The Roman Body Found on Grewelthorpe Moor in 1850: A Reappraisal' in *Britannia* Vol.22 (1991)

Vallance, Edward, *A Radical History of Britain* (Little, Brown; London, 2009)

Wanley, Nathaniel, *The Wonders of the Little World: Or, A General History of Man, Displaying the Various Faculties, Capacities, Powers and Defects of the Human Body and Mind* (W. J. and J. Richardson; London, 1806)

Williams, Neville, *The Life and Times of Henry VII* (Book Club Associates; London, 1984 [1973])

Wilson, David, *Anglo-Saxon Paganism* (Routledge; London, 1992)

Zaleski, Carol, *Otherworld Journeys: Accounts of Near-Death Experience in Medieval and Modern Times* (Oxford University Press; Oxford, 1987)

ZOMBIE CREDITS

Zombie heads with kind permission of Chris Spooner,
http://blog.spoongraphics.co.uk

PAGE 6
Zombie phrenology revealed. (With the kind permission of Andy Pitts,
www.the1948timemachine.com. Check out his store before you go a-hunting,
and get it on a T-shirt!)

PAGE 17
Boudica by the Thames, with Britain's earliest known zombie horse. (With
thanks to Martin Colloms)

PAGE 21
St Patrick – not only armed with a staff, but driving hundreds of snakes
towards you. Indiana Jones need not apply. (Library of Congress, LC-USZ62-
31937)

PAGE 23
King Arthur. N.B. strange women lying in ponds distributing swords is no basis
for a system of government. (Library of Congress, LC-USZ62-133691)

PAGE 27
King Alfred in Pyle's *The Story of King Arthur and His Knights*. Incinerated
baked goods, not shown. (THP)

PAGE 31
Cnut meeting Edmund Ironside. A short while later he slaughtered Edmund's
entire family. (THP)

PAGE 35
King Macbeth – beard and bling, model's own. (Library of Congress,
LC-USZC4-738)

PAGE 37
William the Conqueror – you fat bastard. (THP)

PAGE 39
William Rufus in the forest, arrow in the chest. (THP)

PAGE 40
The death of Thomas Becket: 'Who will rid me of this accursed zombie?' (THP)

PAGE 45
Llewellyn the Great and his tomb. Give him a hand. (Rhion Pritchard)

PAGE 47
Death vs the monks! (With kind permission of the Thomas Fisher Rare Book Library, University of Toronto)

PAGE 49
Statue of William Wallace at Aberdeen – queue to kill me, this way! (Axis12002)

PAGE 51
Edward I. It's Hammer Time! Run away! (THP)

PAGE 53
Edward II. Not dancing the red-hot polka. (THP)

PAGE 59
Robert the Bruce. Last one to England's a lassie! (THP)

PAGE 61
The Black Prince with his captive, the king of France. 'I wanted to be called the Dark Lord, but the name was already taken – so the Black Prince it was.' (THP)

PAGE 63
The death of Wat Tyler, from a nineteenth-century engraving. Horses and armour convincing; dog on the left, not so much. (THP)

PAGE 67
Henry IV. 'Diseased Nature oftentimes breaks forth in strange eruptions.' (Shakespeare, *Henry IV* part 1) (THP)

PAGE 69
Owain Glyndwr. 'I am not in the roll of common men.' (Shakespeare, *Henry IV* part 1) (THP)

PAGE 71
Henry 'Loadsamoney' VII, from *Illustrations of English and Scottish History.* (THP)

PAGE 73

Anne Boleyn. Hat may or may not conceal Voldemort – there's only one way to find out... (With kind permission of the Thomas Fisher Rare Book Library, University of Toronto)

PAGE 75

Henry VIII. Anyone who doesn't sing *I'm Henery the Eighth, I Am* as they approach loses ten points. (With kind permission of the Thomas Fisher Rare Book Library, University of Toronto)

PAGE 77

'Bloody Mary' in her prime. No.1 in the 'All-Time Terrible Tudors' poll. (THP)

PAGE 79

The execution of Mary, Queen of Scots. Blindfold, model's own. (THP)

PAGE 81

Drake accused Thomas Doughty of witchcraft, mutiny and treason on extremely tenuous grounds – the arrival of a sudden storm. Doughty was beheaded. (Library of Congress, LC-USZ62-135589)

PAGE 83

Elizabeth I. Gloriana in Excelsis. (THP)

PAGE 85

The arrest of Guy Fawkes – autograph hunters need not apply. (THP)

PAGE 87

Bradgate House, the home of Thomas Grey, 2nd Marquess of Dorset. (Andrew Norman)

PAGE 89

William Shakespeare. Need a skull for the Yorick scene in *Hamlet*? Bill might well be able to oblige. (Library of Congress, LC-USZ62-80147)

PAGE 91

Pocahontas on her visit to the UK. May or may not sing you a song as she attacks. (Library of Congress, LC-USZ62-8104)

PAGE 93

Sir Walter Raleigh: feeling a bit ruff. (Library of Congress, LC-USZ62-2951)

PAGE 95

James I. I love the smell of burning witches in the morning. (Library of Congress, LC-USZ62-104640)

PAGE 98
Micklegate Bar, where John Bartendale revived. (Library of Congress, LC-DIG-ppmsc-09038)

PAGE 99
View of Victorian Oxford. (Library of Congress, LC-DIG-ppmsc-08764)

PAGE 101
Oliver Cromwell, already fairly scary in life. (THP)

PAGE 102
Signatures on Charles I's death warrant. (THP)

PAGE 103
A plague on both your houses! (THP)

PAGE 104
London's burning. (THP)

PAGE 107
Charles II. A well-dressed zombie should never be without his wig. (With kind permission of the Thomas Fisher Rare Book Library, University of Toronto)

PAGE 109
Nell Gwyn as she appeared in *Beauties of the Court of Charles the Second*. 'Good people, I am the Protestant zombie, not the Catholic one.' (THP)

PAGE 111
Captain Kidd: the poster zombie for Talk Like a Pirate Day. (THP)

PAGE 115
Newton assessing the gravity of the situation. (THP)

PAGE 117
Rob Roy. 'I'm sure I left my sword around here somewhere...' (THP)

PAGE 119
'The heel bone's connected to the foot bone, the foot bone's connected to the ankle bone...' (THP)

PAGE 121
A contemporary sketch of Dick Turpin in his cave. 'I may be a sadistic rapist, coward and scumbag, but the British public love me.' And York, where his corpse may be found ... (THP)

PAGE 125
Dr Johnson, felinophile. (THP)

PAGE 127
Robert Burns. 'A zombie's a zombie for a' that.' (Library of Congress, LC-DIG-ppmsc-07528)

PAGE 131
Nelson in his study. Kiss *this*, Hardy! (Library of Congress, LC-DIG-pga-03656)

PAGE 133
Jane Austen. 'And this is the Flexor Carpi Radialis Muscle...Do pay attention, Mr Darcy!' (Library of Congress, LC-USZ62-103529)

PAGE 135
William Burke. 'Fresh bodies! Get yer fresh bodies 'ere!' (THP)

PAGE 141
Mary Shelley. TEENAGE FEMINIST HIPPIE ELOPES WITH POSH BLOKE AND WRITES BESTSELLING HORROR NOVEL SHOCK! (© Mary Evans Picture Library)

PAGE 143
The Duke of Wellington from a contemporary sketch. I don't know what effect this zombie will have on the enemy – but by God, he terrifies me! (THP)

PAGE 145
Charlotte Brontë. 'Have you washed those hands, Heathcliff?' (Library of Congress, LC-USZ62-135583)

PAGE 149
Isambard Kingdom Brunel. Chain male. (© Mary Evans Picture Library/INS. OF CIVIL ENGINEERS)

PAGE 153
Charles Dickens. It's 8 a.m. and Charles has already breakfasted on a critic and written two and half chapters. (THP)

PAGE 155
Charles Babbage, modfather of steampunk. *Illustrated London News*'s obituary portrait. (Library of Congress, LC-DIG-pga-03656)

PAGE 157
Charles Darwin. 'Mmmm. Creationists are *so* tasty.' (Library of Congress, LC-DIG-ggbain-03485)

PAGE 159
Karl Marx. 'What do you mean, I look like a Monty Python animation?' (Library of Congress, LC-USZ62-16530)

PAGE 161
The phantom of the zombie apocalypse. (THP)

PAGE 163
'Lewis Carroll'. 'Remember what the Dormouse said: Feed Your Head'.
(Library of Congress, LC-USZ62-70064)

PAGE 165
Oscar Wilde. We are all in the gutter, but some of us are looking at the scars.
(Library of Congress, LC-USZ62-2883)

PAGE 167
Queen Victoria. Still not amused. (THP)

PAGE 169
Florence Nightingale. Nurse! The screens, quick! (Library of Congress,
LC-USZ62-5877)

PAGE 171
W.G. Grace. Howzat! ('What do you mean, legbone before wicket?') (THP)

PAGE 173
Lawrence of Arabia. Camels, not shown. (Library of Congress, LC-DIG-ppmsca-19413)

PAGE 175
Ancient Briton, no doubt about to crumble into dust. (THP)

COLOUR SECTION
Plate 1
Scene from the Bayeux Tapestry, zombie version: *Harold Rex Infectus Est.* (THP)

Plate 2
Richard III. 'Now is the winter of our discontent / Made glorious summer by this sun of York; / And all the clouds that lour'd upon our house / In the deep bosom of the carpark buried'. (© The National Portrait Gallery)

Plate 3
Napoleon III. Sacre-bleu, je suis un zombie! Bof! (Walters Art Museum, acquired by William T. Walters, 1876)

INDEX

Aberdeenshire 34, 97

America 80, 90, 92, 151, 156, 168

Anglo-Saxons 18–9, 22, 26, 28, 30, 133

Angus 97, 113

Basingstoke 105

Bentham, Jeremy 138–9

Berwickshire 97

Berwick-upon-Tweed 43

Bodiam Castle 55

Bog Bodies 8, 28, 112, 136–7, 147, 174, 177, 178

Bournemouth 140

British Museum 13, 29, 151, 177

Bronze Age 24

Buried alive 105, 123

Burton-on-Trent 33

Bury St Edmunds 29

Byland 65

Caernarfon Castle 56

Caerphilly Castle 55

Cambridge/Cambridgeshire 16, 18–19, 174

Canterbury Cathedral 8, 40–1, 60, 66–7

Carlisle Castle 56

Chronicle of Lanercost 46

Civil War, The 30, 100

Cladh Hallan 24

Colchester 16

Conwy 44

Cornwall 97

County Antrim 137

County Armagh 99, 137

County Cork 97

County Derry 18, 136–7

County Down 20–1

County Lough 97

Cumbria 50, 56, 176

Dark Ages 23, 30

Decapitation 11, 18, 33

Defoe, Daniel 103, 116

Derbyshire 33, 112

Devon 122

Dissection 120, 129, 134, 138

Dorset 19, 94, 140, 173

Dover Castle 55

Dumfries 126, 134

Duncan I 34

Dunfermline 58–9

East Anglia 29

East Sussex 55

Edinburgh 55, 88, 134–5

Edinburgh Castle 55

Eilean Donan Castle 57

Essex 30, 62, 120

Executions 18, 48–9, 63, 94, 106, 128

Face-down burials 18–19

France 36–7, 38, 44, 60, 74, 76, 78, 87, 92, 94, 97, 110, 130, 142, 164

Glastonbury 22

Gloucestershire 52–3, 97, 170

Hampshire 105, 168

Hangings 99, 100, 111, 120, 129

Henry II 40, 43

Henry III 44, 64

Hereford 33

Iceni 16

Incorrupt corpses 29
Iona 25, 34–5
Ireland 18, 20–1, 74, 94, 106, 134, 136–7
Iron Age 177
John, King 44
Kent 56, 62, 91
Ladies with the Ring 96–7
Leeds Castle 56
Leicestershire 13, 64, 87
Lincolnshire 19, 64
Lindow Man 29, 177
Liverpool 151
Llanwrst 44–5
London 8, 14, 16, 27, 29, 32, 40, 48–9, 54–5, 62, 68, 72–3, 75, 80, 84, 96, 104, 106, 108, 124, 135, 138–9, 148, 151, 154–5, 158, 170, 173
Manchester 123, 151, 177
Map, Walter 33, 46
Melrose 25, 43, 58
Monmouthshire 68
More, Sir Thomas 73
Mummies 24, 123, 151
National Trust 55, 173
Northamptonshire 16, 78
Normandy 36
Northumberland 42
Northumbria 25, 34
Oxford 99, 151
Paisley 46
Panama 80
Peasants' Revolt 62
Peterborough 78
Piracy 110–1
Plague/pestilence 33, 42, 103, 106
Posthumous executions/punishment 86
Preserved bodies 8, 24, 29, 67, 87, 112, 122, 136–7, 146–7, 174, 176–7

Romans 16, 18–9, 33, 147
St Albans 16
St Brigid 20
St Columba 20, 25
St Drythelm 25
St Edmund 29
St Modwenna 33
St Oran 25
St Paul's Cathedral 8, 104, 130, 142, 168
Scandinavia 30, 32, 97
Scotland 13, 14, 22, 24, 25, 34–5, 38, 42, 46, 48–9, 50, 55, 57, 58, 68, 74, 78, 94, 96, 106
Shakespeare, William 34–5, 66, 88–9, 124
Somerset 26, 97
Spain 58, 60, 80, 82, 84, 92, 130, 142
Stirling District 48, 58, 116
Stratford-upon-Avon 88
Surrey 92
Tower of London 14, 54–5, 72–3
Vampires 97, 158
Vikings 26–7
Wales 22, 38, 44, 55, 68, 70, 179
Wars of the Roses 70
Warwick Castle 14, 57
Warwickshire 16, 57, 87, 88, 150
Western Isles 24
Westminster Abbey 8, 32, 50–1, 52, 70, 76, 79, 82, 94, 100, 106, 114, 124, 130, 152, 156, 168
William of Newburgh 42–3, 46
Wiltshire 27
Winchester 26–7, 30, 32, 38–9, 132–3
Windsor Castle 8, 14, 74, 166
Wuthering Heights 146
York/Yorkshire 14, 42, 65, 70, 84, 97, 98, 120–1, 144, 147

www.thehistorypress.co.uk